D1470422

〜

Praying *for* Base Hits

Praying
for
Base Hits

An American Boyhood

Bruce Clayton

UNIVERSITY OF MISSOURI PRESS
COLUMBIA AND LONDON

Copyright © 1998 by

The Curators of the University of Missouri

University of Missouri Press, Columbia, Missouri 65201

Printed and bound in the United States of America

All rights reserved

5 4 3 2   02 01 00 99

Library of Congress Cataloging-in-Publication Data

Clayton, Bruce.

    Praying for base hits : an American boyhood / Bruce Clayton.

      p.   cm.

    ISBN 0-8262-1189-5 (alk. paper)

    1. Clayton, Bruce—Childhood and youth. 2. Kansas City (Mo.)—

Biography.   I. Title.

F474.K253C58   1998

977.8'411043'092—dc21

[B]   98-021276

                                  CIP

♾™ This paper meets the requirements of the
American National Standard for Permanence of Paper
for Printed Library Materials, Z39.48, 1984.

Designer: Stephanie Foley

Printer and binder: Thomson-Shore, Inc.

Typefaces: Adobe Garamond and Korinna

FOR MY WIFE, CARRAH

Contents

Praying *for* Base Hits

1

"They Shot DiMaggio Today"

"**W**hat did you say," I yelled at my father half hysterically. "What did you just say to Mom?"

"They shot Binaggio and Gargotta today. That's what I said," Dad answered gruffly from behind his newspaper. He looked up to gaze without admiration on his sweaty son, who stood before him shirtless, holding a baseball mitt in one hand and a pair of cleats in the other.

"Some gangsters shot Binaggio and Gargotta. Killed them. Why don't you ever pay attention? What did you think I said? Anyway, what do you care about a couple of dagos getting killed?"

Care? I didn't. I couldn't care less about two guys named Binaggio and Gargotta. I'd heard about them. On that April day in 1950 I knew, with all the wisdom an eleven year old could command, that they were hoods, "members of the mafia," kids at school said knowingly. But everyone in the Northeast neighborhood of Kansas City (everyone, that is, except the Italians) mentioned the Mafia knowingly whenever any prominent local

Italian name came up. And that's all I knew about the North Side political boss, Charles Binaggio, and his unfortunate sidekick.

"I thought you said *DiMaggio,* Joe DiMaggio," I replied softly, defensively, angrily.

Dad stared at me for a long moment, his expression shifting between contempt and dismay. He returned to reading the *Kansas City Star,* but not before muttering something about "baseball" and "sports," and was that all I ever thought about.

"What did you do today," my father asked without looking up. I doubted that he really cared. His general indifference, added to a day of very hard work at the Ford Motor Company assembly plant, made him all but oblivious, and resigned, to what I did. It would have surprised him, no doubt pleased him, to learn that I had a clear understanding of his basic rules. Don't get into trouble at school, don't bother him, and don't, under any circumstances, get "in trouble with the law." The last was the eleventh commandment in his bible.

He would not have found it amusing had I chided him about his own brush with crime and jail. Cousins and neighbors could gleefully recall that soon after moving to Kansas City in 1943 from a depressed Missouri farm he had carelessly accumulated a pile of parking and speeding tickets that he simply ignored. One day the police arrived, marched up the front steps, asked whether he was Roy Roosevelt Clayton, and arrested him. They said he would have to go downtown and be held until someone posted bond and arranged to pay all of his tickets.

I had sort of admired him that day. He climbed into the police car with a bit of a hangdog look on his face, but he waved nonchalantly to the curious neighbors, some of whom couldn't suppress a grin. "Roy thought he was still down on the farm where he could just say to hell with the cops! Guess he knows better now," said old Mr. Jim, our next-door neighbor. Mr. Jim, my idol, could say something like that and get away with it. But a lumbering eleven year old who cared only for baseball and goofing off had better keep still.

"Went to school. Played some ball," I answered to his question about how I spent the day. "Practiced the trombone." I lied about the trombone; that fib was mainly for my mother's benefit. She sat close by, quietly peeling potatoes. But she was listening to every word. Nothing got by her.

I started to say "and jacked around with my friends," but caught myself. She fiercely disapproved of any expression or slang that bordered on the obscene. "Gosh" and "gosh darn" and other tame expressions brought stern admonitions about bad language. Those words didn't fool her one bit. She knew they were just a perverse way of taking the Lord's name in vain, of letting the devil and his crowd get their hooks in you. "I don't want to hear you say it; I don't want to hear you talk like that," she warned.

By now I had recovered my emotional equilibrium and was in no danger of defiling God's name or admitting that I had jacked around with my buddies. For one brief, terrible moment my mind had gone reeling. Had some screwball-bastard-son-of-a-bitch shot DiMaggio, Joltin' Joe, the "Yankee Clipper," the greatest ballplayer alive? The Yankee Clipper was right up there, almost, with Babe Ruth, the "Sultan of Swat," and Lou "the Iron Horse" Gehrig, and "the Georgia Peach," Ty Cobb.

DiMaggio! DiMaggio was God in pinstripes. I knew

all about him, knew when he came up with the Yankees, knew how he had "lost" three years serving in the military during World War II, knew how many homers he'd hit and that he had two brothers playing for rival teams. Everything! I'd seen him play on the neighbor's new television set (the only one on the block), listened to radio broadcasters extol his virtues, read about him in the *Kansas City Star,* and stared in wonderment at his picture in *Sport* magazine. I'd dreamed about seeing him in person someday, if the mighty Yankees ever came to town.

Who was better, Joe D. or Ted Williams? DiMaggio or Stan "the Man" Musial? "No doubt about it, it's Joe DiMaggio," said Mr. Jim, who knew all there was to know about baseball. That clinched it for me. But Joe D. was getting old, the experts were saying, and near the end. Injuries had forced him to miss a lot of games in 1949, and he'd had a lousy World Series in the Yankees' victory over the Brooklyn Dodgers. His was a brilliant career. No one could take that away from him. But now, well, the ravages of time had left their mark. Still, for me Joe D. would roam center field forever.

No, nobody had shot DiMaggio. Maybe Mom was right—there was a God. Still, baseball's immortals couldn't be too careful. I recalled Mr. Jim breaking the news about Eddie Waitkus, the Phillies' first baseman, having taken a slug in the stomach from some dame in 1949. "But what was he doing in that strange woman's hotel room?" Mr. Jim said he sure didn't know.

I kept silent about Eddie Waitkus and Joe DiMaggio. My old man, weary from a long day of work, was engrossed in his newspaper or whatever private world he inhabited in his mind. Besides, he hated baseball. All sports. I don't think he'd ever played any games down on that farm around Wakenda.

Mom, also a refugee from the farm, smiled when she heard me say I'd practiced the trombone while she had been away at work all day, making large vats of coffee and serving as cashier at the end of the food line in the Ford Motor Company cafeteria. Music lessons, any kind, were good for you. "They keep kids off the streets" was one of her many maxims and her ready answer when asked about the wisdom of shelling out her hard-earned wages for music lessons.

She had no particular love for the trombone. But she'd played the piano some when she was a girl, and though she couldn't sing three consecutive notes on key, she

1949: Mom and Dad with their first grand-child. I am on the porch, an uncle at age ten.

loved church music, and had ever since she had started, as a child, singing hymns. Later, when times got better after the move to Kansas City, where Mom found wartime work at the Lake City Arsenal making bullets, she bought herself a small electronic organ, put it in the bedroom, and played hymns and sang to herself.

She thought the trombone an odd instrument, but at least it was an improvement over the old, double-ugly, dented school tuba I'd started out on a few years earlier. So I lied about the trombone and didn't say anything about having palled around with my buddies after school and before ball practice.

She was tired; she didn't need to hear the truth. She was a demon for work and was always hatching up some scheme to make extra money—whether it was baking and selling fruitcakes at Christmastime or taking in laundry that she washed in an old-fashioned machine, the kind with the hand-turned wringer. In winter or on rainy days, she hung the washing in the basement. Then she ironed it, folded it, and returned it, sometimes walking and carrying the baskets herself.

She wasn't proud. Not about work or about money. One of her best customers was Jimmy Pointer, who lived around the corner from us in a big stone house, one that was far grander than the humble bungalows of the neighborhood. He was slightly dandified by Northeast's working-class standards, not the sort of person Mom normally approved of—he sported a thin mustache and smoked cigarettes through one of those long, sissified filters. Odder yet, by her standards, he wore a fresh white dress shirt and necktie everyday, even on days he wasn't working. But that gave her more laundry to do, more money to make.

Curses. I dreaded hearing her say I had to go with her to help her tote his laundry. And we always had to go to his back door. But every time I complained she said hush, that the shirts didn't weigh much, and that it wasn't going to kill me to do a little work. Where did I think my allowance and money for music lessons came from? Jimmy Pointer (I never heard him called Mr. Pointer) had some kind of white-collar job. Besides, he paid her good money—he even tipped. So I was to be extra polite to him. Money doesn't grow on trees, you know.

Sometime in the early morning hours of April 6, 1950, a couple of hit men had murdered Charles Binaggio by putting a bullet in his head. His partner in misadventure, Charles Gargotta, zoomed into eternity in the same manner. They were shot at close range in the Club Room of the First District Democratic Club, a holdover from the regime of Kansas City's infamous Tom Pendergast, and in 1950 still a powerful political force in the Northeast part of the city.

The Democratic Club was over on Fifteenth Street, not too far from our house on Thompson Street. The *Kansas City Star,* barely able to control its glee, played up the murders big time. A special afternoon edition blanketed the city with screaming headlines and vivid descriptions of how Gargotta ("a North Side underworld character") and Binaggio, the don of the North Side and the heir of the imprisoned Charles Carollo, met their maker by having their brains blown out. The *Star* crowed, pointing out that back in 1939 the Kansas City mobster Johnny Lazia had been dispatched to the next world in the same way.

Big doings. You bet. Just the sort of thing to stir the imagination of a wide-eyed eleven year old who cared

It was time for baseball practice. I am the one leaning on the taped bat.

only that Joe D. was alive and safe. Rumors swirled around that Binaggio's crowd had their hands firmly planted on President Truman's shoulder. It was no coincidence, some said, that Fifteenth Street was later renamed Truman Road. Even little kids on Thompson Street knew that Truman had owed something to someone named Pendergast, who'd made sure guys like Lazia, Carollo, and Binaggio had police protection to run their rackets—as long as they got out the vote for the Pendergast candidates.

The next day, after school, I jumped on my bike with a pack of Thompson Street kids and raced to the scene of the crime. We wanted to see blood, lots of blood. We expected to see shattered glass and bullet holes everywhere. Blood-splattered bodies, we hoped, would still be sprawled in their chairs or crumpled on the floor. Angry small-time hoods would be hanging around, swearing revenge. We dreamed in technicolor as we pedaled furiously and dodged honking automobiles along Fifteenth Street. You knock off a Binaggio or a Gargotta and you are going to pay. "Oh man, somebody is going to pay." The image of two slain mobsters, whose names had been mere sounds to us before their deaths, now bounced around gloriously in our tiny minds as we counted the ways their deaths would be avenged.

Once there, we found to our disgust that the police had cordoned off the building, covered the windows, locked the doors. There were a couple of squad cars with bored policemen sitting in them. They told us to beat it, to "go on, get out of here." Come on, we shot back, let us have a peek at the Club Room where the mob boys got it. "Who knows, we might be able to find some clues you guys overlooked." We had our copies of Dick Tracy's crime-stopper's book in our hip pockets. The cops weren't amused. "You kids beat it before we call your folks."

We couldn't stay around much longer anyway. It was time for baseball practice. Our season wouldn't begin for another month, but the teams had been picked by our coaches—kids' fathers and men who worked at the steel mill or at one of the meatpacking plants in the East Bottoms and smoked cigarettes or chewed tobacco (but would smack you good if they caught you doing either) and wore overalls and new Yankees or Cardinals baseball caps tilted jauntily to one side. These men were always "Mr. Kinney" or "Mr. Sullivan" or "Mr. Poole."

"Coach" was reserved for any of them who could really throw a ball or hit it hard or had "played pro ball" somewhere up in Iowa or down in North Carolina. We never worked up our nerve to ask any "coach" where he'd played. But some of them—well, you could just tell from the easy way they moved, or by the graceful way they fired the ball back at you if you were idiot enough to get into a game of "burnout" with any of them.

In spring practice they sized us up by hitting fly balls and pitching batting practice. At the end of each session they'd stay and work out various lineups. The year before, on a raw, windy March day in 1949, I had been the last player chosen, one of those baby-fat kids Mr. Kinney put in the game only because 3 & 2 Baseball League rules said he had to. Coaches waited until the game was safely in hand or hopelessly lost before inserting a sure out like me in the lineup. I was so ungainly, so clumsy, that I didn't even merit a regular gray uniform with STA-MAC—short for Standard Maintenance Company—across the front of the shirt.

My uniform, left over from a defunct team, was an ugly bluish purple with BERLE FORD in white lettering. Although I was tubby, this baby-elephant-size suit looked baggy. Half of me hated that uniform; but the other half loved it. I was on a team. I had a glove, an old, flattened first baseman's mitt my older brother had liberated from the United States Navy in 1945. I was also the proud owner of a pair of real baseball shoes, spikes they were called, the kind with metal cleats just like DiMaggio wore.

My father could only shake his head slowly but deliberately when I put on that garish, baggy uniform. "What's your position," he'd usually jab at me whenever he saw me before a game. His words stung, but I tried not to let on. "Right fielder," I told him, trying to sound indifferent. Of course even he, the man from the farm, knew what it meant to be a right fielder, and a substitute one at that.

But I usually didn't give him much of a chance to comment. If lucky, I could escape before he got home from work, knowing that he had no interest in coming to see me play—or ride the bench. I threw my cleats and glove over the handlebars of my bicycle and headed off to the ballpark.

I never told him that I had gone the entire 1949 season without a hit, or even a walk. I had gone to the plate all of four times that summer and struck out every time. Mercifully, no balls had been hit to the substitute right fielder in the billowy blue jersey. No fly balls, that is, until the time a menacing blooper careened my way.

It was during a night game near the heart of Northeast's Little Italy at Fifth and Maple (each team was allotted two games a season "under the lights"). It was cold and drizzly; it was late and the game was about over and Mr. Kinney had pointed to right field. I stood there with goose bumps trying to keep warm by yelling encouragement to our pitcher—one was to "chatter" at all times, the father-coaches told us.

I chattered, "Come on, babe, come babe, just throw a strike, come on babe." I also prayed fervently that no ball would be hit my way. It was dark and the lights were only barely adequate—playing "under the lights" was far less glamorous than I had imagined. The other team got a couple of runners on base. Then the truly awful happened: a pop fly veered off down the right-field line.

I gave chase. But, wouldn't you know it, the ball fell just beyond my reach. I lurched toward it, grabbed it from the damp grass, and stood up, wound up, and threw the slippery ball with all of my might. I flung it toward home plate. The darn ball—sorry Mom—sailed over the first baseman's head, over our bench, and into the stands as the runners raced home. Our shivering fans erupted in a loud groan. Mr. Kinney screamed at me.

"Foul ball," the umpire yelled before turning and signaling the runners to return to their bases. "Just a long strike," someone consoled from our side of the stands. I was cold, but I was dripping with sweat. I was awful. Foul ball or not, everybody at Fifth and Maple that night knew it. The old man was right about the substitute right fielder.

But April 1950 had a different feel about it. I arrived at Lykins Park, four blocks down the street from our house, with a new look. I had grown taller, and leaner. Much of my pudgy fat had evaporated. My arm was stronger. "You look more like a ballplayer," said Mr. Kinney, whose son looked nothing like a ballplayer but got to pitch anyway.

Early in May 1950, a couple of weeks after Binaggio and Gargotta met their maker, a miracle happened. I began hitting the baseball. That winter I started following my mother's admonitions and began praying—for a strong arm, for base hits, for a real mitt, a glove of my own. Of course, one was supposed to pray for forgiveness, for salvation from sin, for life everlasting, for the health and well-being of family members—and for better wages at the Ford plant. One was also to pray earnestly that God would guide those who have "power and dominion over us." I prayed for a STA-MAC uniform and a level swing so that I might smite with my bat those menacing pitchers who had power and dominion over me.

1949: I was
the last player
chosen.

By the time of
this photo,
much of my
pudgy fat had
evaporated.

My prayers were answered. Standing at the plate I could actually see the ball coming at me, see it as though it was arriving in slow motion. I hit Mr. Kinney's best fast ball. But even Mr. Kinney's best hard one had a slight arch in it. How would I do against "real pitching"? The answering fact came early in the spring, in a "practice game" against a rival team, one with a real pitcher. I got a hit. Not a cheap hit, either. No bloop to right field, but an honest clean hit up the middle, right by the pitcher's head.

I was jubilant, though I was cool enough to be nonchalant about it, just like Joe D. But my heart overflowed. Euphoria lingered for at least a week; I would find myself staring off into space reliving that golden moment. The pitcher winds, throws; I see the ball coming toward the plate; it's the size of a grapefruit. I swing. It's a line drive. A hit. I have been in the thrall of that moment for the rest of my life.

Hey! I now understood what all those coaches and fathers had meant when they shouted "keep your eye on the ball," "just meet it," "don't try to kill it." But I had killed it; I'd smacked it right up the middle, whistling it by the pitcher's ear. With that hit a great fear vanished—the dread of never hitting a ball, of not making the team, of forever riding the bench in a big blue uniform, of being the failure my father knew I was.

But could I field? Mr. Kinney had been "trying me out" at third base. Anywhere was fine. I wanted to pitch, of course, but I kept silent. Mr. Kinney saw that I had three characteristics of many third basemen: I was big and slow, but I could throw the ball across the infield— sometimes in a straight line. Determination blazed in my eyes as I trotted out to third in my STA-MAC uniform.

A tendency to look toward heaven when thundering ground balls came right at me gave Mr. Kinney pause, but it was early yet, and if he continued to yell "keep your head down, son," I might just make it.

Every night before going to bed I crouched in the dark, frequently with my ball glove on my hand, and repeated, "Keep your head down, keep your head down." I challenged imaginary batters. Go on, just try to hit one by me. I'd show them. And I would show Mr. Kinney, and Shortcake Durham (my buddy at shortstop), and Leonard "Two Bananas" Tulipanna, STA-MAC's pint-size second baseman.

Twelve days after the two Charlies, Binaggio and Gargotta, got it for good, the New York Yankees opened the 1950 season with a rousing come-from-behind victory over the Boston Red Sox. Batting against the Bosox's skinny, crafty left-hander, Mel Parnell, the Yankee Clipper hit a single, a double, and a triple. Joe DiMaggio was still the greatest. No! No one had shot DiMaggio! And a curse on all those who said Joltin' Joe was washed up. Bring on baseball!

2

Mr. Jim

I loved Mr. Jim. Spring, summer, fall: evening after evening Mr. Jim sat contentedly on the front porch next door and read the *Kansas City Star*, sipped whiskey, smoked cigarettes, talked, fed Oreo cookies to appreciative squirrels, and nodded agreeably to passersby. He was tall and bald with wisps of white hair above his ears. He'd been lanky as a Missouri farm boy, and lean: you could still tell that from his slender shoulders and thin ankles.

"That man's got the skinniest ankles and smallest feet in the world," said my mother many times, and never approvingly. "And look at that stomach. Why, he looks seven months pregnant." He did. Mr. Jim looked like he'd swallowed a bowling ball. But he wasn't fat; he was almost skinny, except for that tummy. In the summer his much commented upon shape was accentuated by his customary front-porch sitting attire: a sleeveless white cotton undershirt. "Too much of that beer," my mother pronounced, and often. "That Jim Strange" was to be a cautionary example of what liquor and laziness

Thompson Street. Mr. Jim's house is on the left, and ours is in the middle.

would lead to in this life.

Oh, she was wrong. Jim Strange (never called James by anyone I ever knew) was Jim to the grownups. But he was always Mr. Jim to me, and to all the kids on Thompson Street. Mr. Jim was a gentleman, a man blessed with an exquisite appreciation of leisure. Hurry somewhere? Not on your life! And around the house, he never lifted a finger.

"I do enough work on the job," he replied to anyone who tactlessly suggested that he might repair the torn screen on the front door or try to monkey with the intricacies of a carburetor. He would no more have fiddled with the water pump on his aging 1946 Ford, grandly and aptly called a "Super DeLuxe Fordor Sedan," than he would have considered taking up bowling or the polka.

In winter he graciously allowed my father to shovel the snow on his front walk; in summer he sat serenely on his front porch while my father, guiding an old push mower, cut his lawn. Later, when working-class affluence allowed for the purchase of a fancy power mower, Mr. Jim retreated inside and closed the windows to blot out the racket of "that infernal machine." It would never have crossed Mr. Jim's mind to suggest that any of us kids cut the grass or do anything he didn't like to do. Here was nobility, largeness of soul, a patrician outlook on life. We knew the meaning of "gentleman" before we could spell the word.

"Now, Roy likes to mow," he would say. And he was right, as always. Dad—fresh from the farm, a true child of the working class, survivor of the depression, and Mr. Jim's junior by fifteen years—loved tinkering with the lawn mower before carefully mowing the yard. He then took dead aim at Mr. Jim's lawn. Our adjoining front yards were little more than postage stamps of earth, and little New York Yankees in the making had beaten the backyards into dirt, but my father insisted on aiming the mower at any standing blade of grass or dandelion.

When the mowing was finished, Mr. Jim turned to Mrs. Strange, Ruby, and asked her to get my dad a cold beer—an offer that came routinely after the completion of any job on any day, hot or cold. Graciousness, generosity, liberality of spirit, that was Mr. Jim up and down and all over.

And mischievousness. He enjoyed knowing about

Mom's unrelenting religious objections to alcohol. If she knew one thing, she knew that a drop of whiskey, wine, or beer plunged the guilty headfirst and howling into the gutter. No liquor entered our house—at least as far as she ever knew. Drink was forbidden, as were dirty words, dancing, smoking, fornication, Sunday movies, and refusal to attend church regularly.

So Dad drank his beer quickly, leaning on the porch banister next to Mr. Jim's chair. Sometimes he drank two beers—quickly. Mowing in Missouri's pulverizing heat in July or August demanded regular drinks of something cold. "And, no," he would frequently yell at my mother, "I'm not going to get drunk." To her, water or iced tea was plenty good enough. "But that Jim Strange always has to have his beer."

Only much, much later (when I was grown and married and about the age my father was then) did I come to wonder whether there was any connection between my father's mowing or doing odd jobs for Mr. Jim and Ruby and the enjoyment of unsanctioned beer. Back then I was a child and thought as a child and that seemingly offhanded offer of beer and a Christmas "snort" only heightened my appreciation for Mr. Jim's grandeur and increased my awareness of the gulf between a gentleman and a worker.

Mrs. Strange—Ruby only to Mr. Jim—was short and round, with ruby red hair and a scarlet temper that erupted now and then. And when it did, oh boy could she get someone told. In this, she was my mother's equal. Don't get either of them riled. Why, a fly wouldn't light on someone they got told.

But mainly Mrs. Strange was as generous as Mr. Jim. And as good-hearted. She took life on the wing, as lightly as a sparrow. She laughed easily and often; salty stories, sayings, or off-color remarks were greeted with grins and guffaws. And could she swear! A drunken sailor had nothing on her. Her bawdy swearing was always full of good cheer.

She greeted mornings with a smile—as soon, that is, as she'd had her coffee and a drag or two on a cigarette. She fixed Mr. Jim's breakfast, packed his lunch, and then chauffeured him to work. Mr. Jim didn't drive, you see. He saw "no damned reason to learn," and he scoffed at anyone who commented on his unmanly decision. "I never go anywhere except to work," he explained to those who stared at him in bewilderment, "and Ruby takes me."

Whether he actually knew how to drive an automobile was unknown, uncommented upon. He was born (sometime around the late 1880s) and raised on a farm, "down around Neosho, Missouri," I had heard him tell my father when they talked about their country boyhoods. Young boys of his generation had come of age in the earliest days of the automobile and became men by learning to roll their own cigarettes, drink hard cider or whiskey out of a mason jar, and drive a Model T Ford. Mr. Jim had mastered the smoking and drinking parts. But driving, well, he saw nothing in that.

He spoke the truth. He seldom went anywhere except to work. Each weekday morning around 6:30, Mr. Jim, lunch pail in hand, got in their aging, commodious Ford and rode off to work sitting beside his Ruby.

Come the first warm days of spring—and always in the summer and during the still-hot afternoons of fall—Mrs. Strange would take a six-pack of Budweiser out of the icebox. (The iceman had all but disappeared, but everyone still called those newfangled first refrigerators *iceboxes*.) She packed the beer in a cooler filled with ice and drove off to wherever Mr. Jim was working. Her provider would be hot and thirsty.

Mr. Jim was an ironworker, one of that breed of hearty, tough, hard-drinking men. He was a rivet thrower who stood below the men balanced on the steel beams high above the ground. He heated the rivets. When they were glowing white-hot from the fire, Mr. Jim removed them with tongs and hurled them skyward to be caught in a can and hammered into the steel.

A rivet thrower was an aristocrat among ironworkers, a prince, in demand wherever the mighty buildings or bridges of iron and steel went up. Highly skilled rivet

Ruby Strange wasn't like other women. She made the waves of sound dance.

throwers could count on steady paychecks. In boom times, construction companies across the land advertised for rivet throwers and brought them to the job.

Mr. Jim worked with fire. The sun, the flames, a fondness for the bottle, and the flying, white hot rivets had given Mr. Jim's face a scarlet hue. At quitting time, he was in need of a cooling ale.

"She babies that man," my mother complained to anyone in earshot.

"Jim brings home the bacon, so I bring out the beer," Mrs. Strange announced from time to time to no one in particular, in the same assured tone with which my mother said that we should all "pray without ceasing." Mrs. Strange got no argument from me or any other of the grubby little boys who often on summer afternoons sat on the curb waiting to greet Mr. Jim.

On slow days, or extra hot ones when we'd played baseball till we dropped, or when Mrs. Strange was entrusted with "watching us" while our parents worked, we piled in the backseat of their old humpbacked palace on wheels and rode along with her when she went to pick up Mr. Jim. I don't know why, but he always seemed genuinely happy to see a passel of dirty-faced kids. We'd get a wink, or a smile, or a question. "You boys play ball today?" And had any of us "really put the fat part of the bat on the ball?" Or had we given that skinflint pharmacist Mr. Pierce a hard time? He hoped so.

"Has anyone heard how the Yankees did today? Who will be on the mound tonight for the Kansas City Blues?" Often he was whimsically testing us, keeping us on our toes. He knew the answers to his questions. On the job, the men talked baseball, and Mr. Jim knew everything about the game of my shimmering dreams. As a young ironworker, roaming the country for work, he'd helped build Yankee Stadium and had seen Babe Ruth and Lou Gehrig and other immortals play. Such was but one part of the grandeur that was Mr. Jim.

Now, we weren't to believe any of that horseshit about Ruth not being a good outfielder. Mr. Jim knew better. And we were to remember that the Babe had a great arm. Mr. Jim had seen the Babe gun down runners at third or home when they foolishly tested his arm. He'd been a pitcher, you know, and pitchers have to have strong arms. And we weren't to fall for any of that baloney about the Babe being a slow or lazy base runner. The man could hit, but he could also run. "You boys remember that." I have.

Seated comfortably in the car, Mr. Jim would down a cold one. He chivalrously asked about Mrs. Strange's day and wondered what was on the super table. After that, he usually rode along in peaceful silence, sipping his beer, seemingly oblivious to our backseat horsing around. He and Mrs. Strange were the only adults we knew who didn't seem to mind our madcap habit of hitting each other on the arm or rubbing our knuckles hard on someone's head to give them a "Dutch rub." I honestly believe they enjoyed it all.

In between quizzing us about the Blues or what we thought of the year's crop of Yankee hopefuls, particularly that new kid from Commerce, Oklahoma, Mickey Mantle, Mr. Jim quietly refreshed himself with cold beer. If the traffic was heavy and the job was some distance from home, he might put away most of the six-pack.

Like an archdeacon, he was the soul of ritual. On returning home to their modest two-bedroom bungalow on Thompson Street, he sat down to supper. Year-round:

pork chops, fried chicken, pot roast, brown gravy, white bread, butter, potatoes, and vegetables cooked long and slow until they melted in your mouth. In the summer: fresh sliced tomatoes, fruit, corn on the cob, green beans, peas in creamy sauce—all washed down with a glass or two of cold milk. When he finished, Mrs. Strange drew Mr. Jim a tub of water and laid out a clean washcloth and towel. In time, he emerged in his pajamas and headed regally for his chair on the front porch. He carried the evening newspaper in one hand, a glass of whiskey in the other.

Saturdays were sacred. He arose at a leisurely hour, ate a country breakfast of bacon and eggs and biscuits, and put on one of his two suits—in summer, a light gray one; in cooler weather, a dark gray double-breasted wool suit. Even on the hottest dog days of late July or August, Mr. Jim wore a long-sleeved white shirt and a wool tie—and not one of those pre-tied, clip-on jobbies Dad wore whenever he had to put on a suit.

Mr. Jim had two hats. In summer he wore a straw boater, tilted neither to the left nor to the right. Leave it to Mr. Jim to look good in a straw boater; no one else in the neighborhood even owned one, as far as we knew. On fall days when there was a hint of chill in the morning air Mr. Jim donned a soft gray fedora.

Properly dressed—and did he cut a figure in working-class Northeast—Mr. Jim walked to the corner tavern, the Monroe Inn, down on Independence Avenue. No, it cannot, in truth, be said that he walked. He sauntered, he moseyed, in the relaxed manner of a Missouri farm boy on his way to town or church. He waved obligingly to neighbors sitting on their front porches, reading the newspaper, sipping a second cup of coffee, and lazily watching the world go by. Mr. Jim's weekly morning stroll—all of four short city blocks—was the sum and substance of his weekend physical exertion. His Saturday morning perambulation added sheen and glory to the princely Mr. Jim.

Once inside the dark, friendly confines of the corner tavern, Mr. Jim treated himself to a bracing boilermaker—a shot of whiskey and a beer chaser. Now and then, he took an egg in his beer—"for strength," he would say in answer to our incessant questions, and perhaps for luck as he sat down for some serious card playing. He and his cronies played poker, five-card stud, and anted up sometimes with silver dollars but usually with chips. The neighborhood cops could be trusted to have better things to do than bust a friendly game of poker, but gambling chips were convenient. When pestered about whether he and his pals ever spiced up their game and allowed the dealer to announce, say, that one-eyed jacks or deuces were wild, he chuckled, saying, "No, this was a man's game."

Sometime early in the afternoon, Mr. Jim and the Saturday morning gang declared it a day. He preferred to stop at a designated time, usually right after lunch. "Quit at the right time, boys," he told us when we asked eagerly about his card playing. "Don't keep playing just because you're winning. The cards can turn against you. And don't quit just because you're losing. Show the other fellows at the table some respect."

He did not walk home. He wouldn't have walked back under any circumstances or in any weather, and, of course, by midday he was usually too far gone in his cups to walk in a dignified manner. No one ever saw Mr. Jim lurching about in the stumblebum fashion of some of the neighborhood drunks. Anyway, Mr. Jim pronounced it unhealthy to walk in the hottest part of the day. The bartender telephoned Mrs. Strange to say that Mr. Jim was ready to come home. Down the hill she drove to pick up her provider.

On sultry, lazy days we'd hitch a ride with her down to the avenue en route to the ballpark or to Mr. Pierce's drugstore, or we'd ride along just to have something to do. Usually, Mr. Jim was waiting at the door when we drove up. When he wasn't, Mrs. Strange would wait patiently, drawing slowly on a dangling cigarette, humming a few bars from the top songs on the Hit Parade. When any of us piped up, "Where's Mr. Jim?" or showed signs of restlessness, she would usually answer, often with a lilt in her voice, "Well, we're not going anywhere, anyway, are we boys."

Like Mr. Jim, she had a soul blessed with patience; hurry and rush were foreign to her nature. (Nobody seemed to be in much of a rush in those days—except Mom when my father dawdled getting ready for church.) Mrs. Strange smoked her Lucky Strikes casually, flicking the ashes out the car window. Life amused her. If Mr. Jim was slow coming out she lit another Lucky Strike—she got more pleasure from taking a slow drag than anyone I've ever known, then or since. If Mr. Jim wasn't in sight, she reckoned he'd had perhaps one too many and was slow getting his coat and hat on and settling up with the barkeep or his gambling buddies.

On extra hot days when we started to squirm or got too rough hitting each other or asked, "What's happened to Mr. Jim?" she'd turn and say with a wink, "Yeah, goddamn it, what the hell's he doing in there, taking a shit, shave, and a shampoo?" She'd have another smoke.

Women and nice girls didn't swear in those days. I'd seldom heard women cuss. I didn't like it when they did. My tiny brain told me, women couldn't cuss right. When they cussed they sounded like they were trying too hard, trying to be something they weren't. But Mrs. Strange wasn't like other women. There was some magic about her. She made the waves of sound dance. Her voice, even when she tried to sound gruff, had a lilt, a lyricism. I think it was because she was completely innocent of meanness—or guile, or envy and deception, or hungering desire to be anything she wasn't, or anywhere else. Mr. Jim and Thompson Street suited her just fine. Nor did dogma, religious or racial, corrupt her mind. Malice was a stranger to her nature.

Sitting on the street curb talking baseball or walking home from the movies or from ball practice—anywhere, that is, out of earshot of adults—one of us kids would say, out of the blue, "Yeah, what the hell's he doing in there, taking a shit, shave, and a shampoo."

It had to be said just right. We repeated it over and over again to get the proper inflection. "A shit, shave, and a shampoo." The tone, the cadence, the volume—we listened with the ear of Toscanini or of Kansas City's own maestro, Hans Schwieger. Sometimes we thought we got it, or got close. But we never did. At school, in study hall, or in class when the teacher turned to face the blackboard, we would punch each other in the ribs and murmur solemnly, "Yeah, goddamn it, what the hell's he doing in there, taking a shit, shave, and a shampoo?"

Years later, after I had become a balding, bearded professor, I survived many a tedious faculty meeting by daydreaming about Mr. Jim and Mrs. Strange. Such golden memories were unseen but felt rays of sunshine in a room groaning with graying, ponderous pedagogues. And, oh, the number of times I've yearned to yell out when some tweedy-coat failed to show at the appointed time, "Yeah, goddamn it, what's he doing, taking a shit, shave, and a shampoo?" Mrs. Strange wouldn't approve. Mr. Jim would.

Some Saturdays, Mr. Jim, deep in his cups, needed a hand. Everyone knew the unwritten code. Mrs. Strange was to stay seated in the car. We were to stay put, too. The bartender or one of Mr. Jim's cronies from the tavern would assist him with a steadying hand at his elbow and help him into the car. After driving him home, Mrs. Strange would ask, did he need any help? If he did, he preferred accepting a hand from my dad, if he was around, or from any male neighbor. I would have been happy to have offered Mr. Jim a helping arm for that short distance from the car to the house. It would have been an honor, but children and teenagers were not even to notice that Mr. Jim was heavy or shaky of foot.

On most Saturdays he was able to navigate under his own power. His gait might be a trifle unsteady, his face flushed, redder than usual, but he was in control. On those afternoons, he returned our admiring glances, greeting us warmly with, "Afternoon, boys."

No matter how much he'd had to drink that morning, neither his tone of voice nor the expression on his face gave the slightest hint of how his luck had run at cards. So, we'd always ask him, "How'd you do this morning, Mr. Jim? Any luck?" "Not bad, boys," meant he'd won a little money, perhaps a lot. An accompanying sly grin signaled he'd hadn't done too badly at all. "Not too good, boys," required no explanation. I remembered he always said a good poker player kept his winnings and losings to himself.

His Saturday ritual was not over. He put on his pajamas and went straight to bed, "to sleep off that whiskey," said my mother. Mr. Jim stretched out for his nap in the front bedroom, the one facing the street. On warm days, he left the window open and the shade up to catch any fleeting cool breezes. Passersby, if they were of a mind to, could look in and see him dozing comfortably on his back, clad in his pajama bottoms and undershirt, his protruding stomach in full view. The only sound to be heard from within was the voice of Larry Ray, announcing the Blues game on the radio.

Mr. Jim would no more have napped in his clothes than my mother would have entered that den of iniquity, that "beer joint" on the corner. My father didn't mow on Saturday afternoons. Kids visiting Thompson Street, hoping to get up a baseball game or at least have a serious game of catch to work on their control or their curve ball, learned not to yell outside his window.

After his nap, he took an early, light supper. Then he assumed his place on the front porch—still in his pajamas—with a cup of coffee and a cigarette, and reproached the *Kansas City Star* for not putting out a Saturday evening edition. He remarked on the weather and greeted my mother rocking in our front porch swing or tending to the honeysuckle on the porch trellis. He yawned, "Hello, Roy," and my father knew that he could now begin mowing or hammering or making whatever racket his work required.

Saturday evenings, Sunday afternoons, weekday evenings were all the same during those languid warm days from late March to early October. Mr. Jim occupied his chair. Mrs. Strange and her sister, Mabel, who dropped in for extended stays now and then, sat on the porch smoking, sipping a drink, listening to songs wafting out from the radio inside.

Their porch was a magnet for young and old. My dad stood by Mr. Jim's chair, leaning on the porch rail. Mr. Cavender, from down the street, ambled up for a sit and some good talk. Elmer was always in his work clothes—bib overalls, with a railroad engineer's cap on his head and a red bandanna around his neck. His hand was never far from his trusty railroad regulation pocket watch. Did you want to know what time it was? Ask Elmer Cavender, he'd tell you down to the second.

Occasionally, Mr. Czar, a trim, handsome, square-jawed carpenter from several houses down, would appear. He never said much; he liked to listen, he said. Sometimes, Mrs. Czar, Harold's mom, came to sit. Pearl Cavender, Elmer's wife and Edwin's mom, seldom did; "Pearly" was frail, sickly. When she wasn't cleaning—and recleaning—their tiny spick-and-span house, she sat for hours on her front porch, rocking in the glider, dreaming and talking wistfully about how much she wanted to return home to Mississippi. I don't think Mr. Cavender ever took Pearly back there, however.

The grownups talked politics—Truman, and hadn't he shown everybody in 1948! After Harry left office and Eisenhower came along, most of Thompson's front-porch Democrats agreed with Dad, who said he couldn't vote against prosperity—he had to vote for Ike. Times were good and getting better. That's why they liked Ike. Adlai Stevenson was a Democrat, but a man who read too many books and sounded like someone "who was too big for his britches"; he was no Truman. The only dissenter was the postman, who said Stevenson read important books, and Ike didn't, and probably didn't even like books, and was a Republican, remember.

They chin-wagged over wages, unions, benefits, working hours, layoffs, strikes, pickets, scabs—those no good "sons-of-bitches." Mr. Jim hated going to union meetings, but he loathed scabs and wanted to know all about elections and gossip down at the meeting hall. Dad, usually laconic, could become quite eloquent on all that Walter Reuther had done for the automobile workers. Mr. Cavender, when he wasn't insisting on picking tunes on his mandolin or setting someone straight on just exactly how many miles it was from Kansas City to Boonville or Liberty or some such place no one wanted to go to, talked up the wonders of the Brotherhood of Locomotive Engineers.

Mr. Czar, Elmer and Pearly Cavender, Mr. Jim, Mabel, Mrs. Strange, Mom, Dad—they knew all about the cost of living. They were the working class, but they never talked about anything like that. Didn't need to. They may have been aware of class, but they would no more have thought of using such highfalutin expressions as "class conflict" or the "proletariat" than they would have considered jumping off the Kansas City Power and Light building. They had a vague idea about who Karl Marx was. Wasn't he "Rooshun"? They hated Communism. Socialism was no better. "Just watered-down Communist claptrap," Dad said, the same way "Pepsi was watered-down Coca-Cola." Marx, Stalin, Mussolini, Hitler were just so many crackpots to the front-porch philosophers of Thompson Street.

They all knew they were better off, that they were eating better, dressing better, than at any time in their lives. "I live better than the old kings of England," my father

My hero, Mr. Jim, charms my baby daughter.

proclaimed. They knew they'd never get rich—they didn't expect to—but they thought their children, at least those who didn't go smash on alcohol or somehow manage to end up in jail, might just do all right.

Mr. Jim didn't care about any of that. When the talk got deep, or a political argument threatened to get out of hand and people started yelling at each other, he'd beat a hasty retreat into the house to listen to the ball game or, by the mid-1950s, watch their new television.

I didn't pay any mind to any of that grown-up stuff either. I knew that Mr. Jim's disdain for such conversation was yet another sign of his understanding of what mattered in life. He wanted to talk baseball, not unions or politics; he said he didn't much care for music either. This he was likely to announce adamantly whenever Mr. Cavender said he could walk down to his house and get his mandolin.

Mr. Jim loved baseball. The other adults didn't. I did. And I loved hearing him talk about having worked on some of the big new iron and steel buildings and having seen the Babe play, and Lou Gehrig, "the Iron Horse," and Tony "the Wop" Lazzeri, and Bill Dickey, and Herb Pennock—there was a pitcher Mr. Jim loved. In St. Louis, while on a big job, Mr. Jim had seen the Cardinals' Gas House Gang play and the brothers Dean, Dizzy and Paul. And Jimmie Foxx, Mel Ott— Mr. Jim had seen them, too. And Ted Williams and Joe DiMaggio when they were in their prime.

"How many home runs did Babe Ruth hit?" That was Mr. Jim's first question to any new kid, clean- or dirty-faced, who appeared on his porch. If you could bark out the answer—714—you had earned the right to sit and talk baseball. And field other questions: what year did the Babe hit sixty home runs? Remember, boys, it was 1927. "Any team ever better than those 1927 Yankees?" Nope.

Who held the record for most consecutive games played? If you knew it was "the Iron Horse," then you should know how many games in that streak—2,130. Tougher: who did Gehrig replace in the Yankee lineup? Answer: Wally Pipp. "What ever happened to Wally Pipp, Mr. Jim?" Oh, he played some for the Yankees and then for some other team. Poor Wally Pipp.

Who was the last player to hit .400? Ted Williams. You're right, but what year was it? Clue: the same year DiMaggio hit in fifty-six consecutive games. And what was Williams's average that year, 1941? Don't know? Look it up. You'll find it was .406. "And remember, boys, Williams went out with a bang. Played both games of a doubleheader on the last day of the season and hit the thunder out of the ball."

How many major-league hitters, do you suppose, had been killed by a pitched ball? A hundred, fifty, twenty-five? Just one: Ray Chapman of the Cleveland Indians. "What year was that, Mr. Jim?" In 1920, in a game against the Yankees. Carl Mays was pitching. "Chapman died the next day, poor bastard."

Here was Mr. Jim's favorite: "Who was the only man ever to pull off an unassisted triple play in the World Series?" Don't know? Mr. Jim chuckled. Go look it up. "Oh, I'll tell you," Mr. Jim answered if anyone looked sheepishly at the floor or shook his head in dismay at his own ignorance. "Bill Wambsganss. In the 1920 World Series." Wambsganss played for the Cleveland Indians and had seen his teammate Ray Chapman get fatally beaned. "Do you know who the Indians played that year to win the World Series?" This was a tough one to remember: it was the Brooklyn Robins—"not the Dodgers, the Robins."

What a wonderful education Mr. Jim handed out free of charge. I didn't know it, none of us did, but we were being taught to know history, to savor and love the past; better yet, to respect it, to know that immortal men had walked the land—or, to be more precise, hit home runs, run the bases, gotten hit in the head and died, performed unassisted triple plays and other acts of magic. Mr. Jim reckoned that one of us just might play ball in the big leagues someday. I glowed from head to toe when he said that.

Mr. Jim was my front-porch Socrates, introducing me to the beauty of baseball as an idea; Mr. Jim was my Aristotle, instilling in me a love of facts. Who was it who pulled off that only unassisted triple play in World Series history? Bill Wambsganss of the Cleveland Indians, and they beat the Brooklyn Robins, remember. Mr. Jim, though he'd snort at the very mention of what I'm going to say, helped to prepare me for the day when I came to love knowledge for its own sake. He taught me to see, though it would take years to fathom any of this, that history, baseball history, but history nonetheless, rooted us and told us who we are.

3

"Shun the Very Appearance of Evil"

B oth of my grandmothers were named Minnie. Minnie Jane Gray married Frederick Marvin Gilbert, and Minnie Bell Workman united with William Valentine Clayton. All were born and grew up, farmed and raised families, and lived out most of their days in and around Wakenda, Missouri, down near Carrollton, in the western part of the state.

Back before the white man came, the mighty Sioux and Osage tribes had hunted and fished and made war in the hills and plains of what would become Carrollton, Waverly, Blue Mound, and Wakenda. The chiefs and medicine men chanted praises to Wah'kon-tah, the Great Mystery. Later, when descendants of the conquering white folks came with names like Gray and Gilbert and Workman, the newcomers said, yes, Wakenda is a fine name for a town and the nearby creek. And so Wakenda got its name. But soon nobody remembered why, and nobody thought of their little dot on the map as the home of any Great Mystery.

Minnie and Fred Gilbert were farm folks who found

the answer to all of life's mysteries in the Bible. They were hardworking people who knew the value of a dollar because they seldom got their hands on more than a few at one time. Neither of them went further than the eighth grade; but, like Minnie and William Clayton, they knew a lot and survived because they did. They knew how to manage their small farm and how to live on the bounty it provided. They knew how to lay by and store for the cold and rainy days that were sure to come, whether you were ready for them or not.

Minnie Jane Gray was strong in the faith of the Wakenda Church of Christ. She took Fred Gilbert as her husband because he was a solid man, a good, plain man, lean with a farmer's honest face, a country face. That homely nose didn't bother her one bit. He was a religious man and could, when the roads washed out and Bro. Robert Brumback or Bro. Jim Campbell couldn't make his way to Wakenda, and there was no one else ready with a word of inspiration, deliver a passable "lesson" to the forty or fifty faithful souls of the church. That he

Wakenda,
1940s.

Minnie and
Fred Gilbert
were farm
folks.

sang a trifle off-key didn't bother anyone—judge not, lest
ye be judged—and didn't keep him from taking his turn
at leading the singing.

For some reason he always said "foldbill" when he
meant billfold. In the evening when chores were done,
he enjoyed reading the Bible or thumbing though the
Saturday Evening Post. He kept the *Farmer's Almanac* and
the Monkey Ward's catalog near at hand. On Saturday
nights he pulled his chair up close to their Philco radio and
tapped his toe quietly to the Blackwood Brothers, "direct
from Nashville's Grand Ole Opry." No one could lay a

Grandpa Gilbert: a solid man, a good, plain man.

patch on them when it came to singing "Amazing Grace" or "When the Roll Is Called Up Yonder." Fred and Minnie Gilbert never had much, and they never knew how much they didn't have. They were at ease in Wakenda, their Zion of a hundred and fifty or so farm folks.

Grandpa Gilbert died during one bitterly cold February in 1948, the same year Babe Ruth died, and Mr. Jim said there would never be another ballplayer that good, and I thought there'd never be another grandpa that good either. The church building was cold, but nothing, not tingling toes or icy fingers, stopped a country funeral. Bro. Fred Gilbert was one of those who stood on the "Rock of Ages," and that was a fact. And he knew that faith without works is dead. Once he'd put on the full armor of righteousness, after a spell of wildness in his youth, he never even thought of taking it off. Stand back,

Satan! Grandpa Gilbert was bound for the glory land.

Death is all bleakness and mystery to children. What do you do when someone dies? Stand around and watch the adults. Do what they do, do what they say. When they cry, you cry. Like everyone else, I marched solemnly by Grandpa Gilbert's open casket. This was everyone's last chance to "view the body" and fix the face, the hair, the eyes—Grandpa's nose—permanently in their mind's eye. "To remember him as he was in life." This was said of a dead man. The undertaker had done a mighty fine job, folks said. But to a scared nine year old who remembered the times his Grandpa had dug into his overalls pocket and fished out a dime and said I was to go "up town" and buy myself a bottle of pop and a Baby Ruth candy bar, Grandpa Gilbert looked like he had turned to stone.

Grandma Gilbert's house after the flood.

The cemetery was colder yet; I feared I might turn into stone. The ground was frozen. The grave diggers, local men with calloused hands, had earned their pay hacking at the sad, grudging earth. At the grave site, Brother Campbell, from up around Excelsior Springs, led the bereaved in a hymn sing and talked about heaven and the rewards coming to anyone who attended church regularly and kept the Commandments.

Three years later, the rains came and the Missouri River leapt out of its banks and marched through the fields and invaded Wakenda. Grandma Gilbert got out safely, but when the floodwaters had crested, the only way "to take a look," Dad announced as the water lapped at our feet, was by motorboat. Our driver took us right up to the side of her house; we bent over and looked through the tops of the windows; several had broken under the pressure of the muddy water. Some of Grandma's prized possessions bobbed languidly in the water, without a care in the world.

By the time that ocean of the Missouri River had ebbed back into its boundaries, most of Grandma's furniture and pictures, and Grandpa's Philco radio, had been ruined. The iron cookstove was all right; so was the potbellied heat stove in the front room. Mildew had started growing on the walls. Mud was everywhere. Dad shoveled it out and said it would take a month of fresh air to get rid of that stench.

Where was Great-Grandpa's uniform, I asked? The old blue one, the one he'd worn in the Civil War, the faded one Grandma kept in a big box at the back of her bedroom closet and would only let me look at. No one knew. The grownups had more important things on their minds, like mud. Don't worry about it, Grandma told me. Just remember that her daddy, Thomas M. Gray, had enlisted and fought for the Union and voted for Abraham Lincoln both times. Young Tom Gray high-tailed it to Carrollton and enlisted in the Sixty-fifth Missouri Regiment. After serving his two-year term he enlisted in the Fourth Missouri Provisional Regiment and stayed in until the end of the war. It was his proudest time, Grandma told me. But what happened to that faded uniform?

Oddly, Dad seemed not to care. His mind was on grown-up matters as he shoveled mud and helped Grandma Clayton clean up her house as well. Tough decisions had to be made. Grandma Clayton, a flinty old widow with many years ahead of her and long accustomed to living alone, said she would be just fine. "Help me clean up and I'll be able to take care of myself." Wakenda suited her. She had eighty acres of good Missouri River bottomland she wanted to keep her eye on. That and her tenant who farmed the land and divided up the profits from the yield.

But Grandma Gilbert waved good-bye to Wakenda and moved to Kansas City to be near her only child and her family. Mom and Dad carted what was left of her belongings to the city and fixed her up in a small apartment on the first floor of a big house across the street from us.

Grandma was getting on. The end was near. But death held no terrors, no sting, for her. She welcomed it for herself. She had raised her family and lived out her days in righteousness. She had kept the Commandments, never taken off the armor of righteousness. Grandpa Gilbert was in Heaven, and she would be joining him in the sweet by-and-by.

Her affairs were in order, all tidied up. She didn't get much for the flood-soaked house in Wakenda, but enough to make do. She had her "burial money." She didn't want "to be a bother" to anyone when her time came and Jesus called her home. She kept her small stash—all of a couple hundred dollars—primly pinned inside the top of her dress right next to her hanky.

Grandma's money—its location and amount known to one and all among family, kinfolks, and church members by the dozen—was a fact of life, as much a part of life as sore throats and earaches and strikes. Grandma's burial money was available for short-term loans to her immediate family, but only for pressing needs. If your pockets were empty and you had no grocery money and your kids—her grandchildren or their cousins—were in danger of going hungry or not having a decent pair of shoes for school, or you had to make a car payment to keep them from coming to take the car, then go talk to Grandma Gilbert. No interest. No carrying charges. But rules. Borrowers had to explain their needs and listen patiently as she said, "This money has got to be paid back. This is my burial money." She would need it "when my time comes, and it's coming pretty soon."

How many times did those tightly folded twenty-dollar bills change hands in the family and provide a small shot in the arm to Kansas City's economy? Many. Did the money always get paid back? It did. Maybe not immediately; maybe not directly out of the borrower's thin "foldbill." Mom and Dad stepped in silently on more than one occasion and saw to it that Grandma Gilbert's Fort Knox maintained its proper level.

Grandma was short, slender, and frail, and never more so than after Grandpa died, the floodwaters rose, and she moved to a city that remained foreign to her until the end. She was meek and mild, but she didn't budge one iota on matters of faith.

If the weather was the least bit favorable, she assumed her favorite spot on her front-porch swing. Coming home from Lykins Park, I passed right by her porch. And stopping off for a glass of water or lemonade was one of summer's treats. She sat contentedly reading her Bible or the *Saturday Evening Post,* but she prized visitors, even sweaty boys and girls, and wanted to know how we were doing in school. She urged us to avoid bad companions and idleness.

She often had a hymnbook handy and liked to hum or quietly sing her favorites, both the verses and the chorus. The hymns were poetry and as relevant to life's problems as verses from the Bible. The problem with most folks was they weren't seeking "Higher Ground"—they weren't pressing on the upward way, gaining new heights every day—or moving onward as Christian soldiers or standing in the shadow of "the Old Rugged Cross."

I liked to stop off at Grandma's house or wander over to join her for talk or a quiet hymn sing. "Rock of Ages" and "Leaning on the Everlasting Arms" were favorites, up there with "What a Friend We Have in Jesus." Sung in a dolorous, dirgelike way, the latter caused Grandma to wipe a tear from her eyes—and nod that here was truth. What would bring back the smiles? A rousing version of "Stand Up, Stand Up for Jesus." Try singing that one when you're depressed, or trying to get yourself out of a pout. Let the chorus rip. You'll feel better.

Grandma was a natural alto. If we pitched the songs low enough, I could get by with singing the lead. If she was in the mood to sing the soprano, I'd sing bass.

Despite warm encouragement, I could never muster the courage to give the tenor part a try. One can look and sound foolish trying to sing tenor, especially if there's just the two of you sitting on the front porch on a quiet, warm afternoon with the neighbors nearby.

Don't be fooled by Grandma Gilbert's small stature or unassuming appearance. She had opinions. Man, she had opinions. When she overheard cuss words, even a mild "damn," sometimes even a quiet "darn it," or looked out on young women in short shorts or tight sweaters or any revealing clothing, she pronounced her verdict. "It's just Sodom and Gomorrah, that's all there is to it, Sodom and Gomorrah!" She waited expectantly for sinners to be turned into pillars of salt. "That's what happened to Lot's wife. She disobeyed God. It wouldn't surprise me one bit to see it happen to some sinners around here."

"Where is Sodom and Gomorrah, Grandma?"

I should have known that from Sunday school, but if I didn't I was to look it up in the Bible. And my buddies and I should read it carefully—or we just might turn into pillars of salt. But her eyes couldn't resist twinkling when she pronounced such possible judgments on her grandson and his grubby pals.

When any of us grimaced or made an angry or sullen face at any of her pronouncements she automatically responded with a smile—and an admonition: "What if your face were to freeze with that look on it. Now you wouldn't want that, would you?" No, Grandma, we certainly wouldn't.

Of course, she frowned on Mr. Jim and Mrs. Strange and their drinking and smoking and failure to be in church on Sunday. And Old Man Pierce, the druggist? "Why, his god is money. He'll be sorry someday. But by then it will be too late. You boys mark my words."

This world was not for Grandma. She had no intention of getting adjusted to this vale of tears. She'd thank you to remember that. She had minimal interest in reading either the morning or the afternoon newspapers—both merely confirmed that "there's a lot of wickedness going on around here." And the daily fifteen-minute tribulations of Stella Dallas, or Backstage Wife, or any of the heroines of the radio soap operas, mattered not a fig to her, she said. But now and then she listened—"just to pass the time."

That new thingamajig called television held no charms whatsoever. Watching TV shows was too much like going to the movies. She was onto Satan. He didn't fool her one bit. Television was the devil's subtle way of softening people up, persuading them to take the next giant step into sin—and traipse off to the movies.

She never reconciled herself to my mother's giving in and allowing me to go to the movies, "but only on Friday nights." Going on Sunday, the Lord's Day, would have been far, far worse, but going on Fridays or Saturdays was sinful, too, and there were "no two ways about it."

For all of my Friday night moviegoing, she spoiled me rotten, slipping nickels and dimes to me. Knowing my fanatical fondness for oranges, she never let Mom go to the grocery store without instructions to bring home a bag of oranges. How many times did Grandma get up from her porch swing and go in and get an orange for me and then peel it? Don't tell me. I only know this: everybody should have a Grandma Gilbert.

And how did I repay her? By sitting on the front porch with her and eating an orange or a popsicle or a fudgesicle; by singing hymns with her; by reciting Bible verses

I had memorized in Sunday school class and Vacation Bible School—all that, and keeping my minor moral transgressions and growing fondness for the things of this world well hidden. I never told her that any of her nickels and dimes went into the pinball machines at Frank's Restaurant.

"Grandma, do you have anything good to drink, something cold? We're thirsty."

She had lemonade, or could make some. She had a jug of water in the icebox. No, my buddies and I thirsted after something better than water. "Lemonade is too sweet. Don't you have nothing else?"

She was an extra good hand at making iced tea. She knew just when to pour cups of sugar into the hot tea and just how long it needed to cool off. But we didn't have time to wait.

"Just hold your wild horses for a moment and I'll get you a glass of cold water," Grandma said.

But all of this was our preliminary sparring to set the stage for saying that what we really craved was pop, soda pop. A Coca-Cola, or a Dr Pepper, or an RC Cola. But she didn't keep any such drinks. They were "too expensive" and "not good for you."

She knew we were setting her up for some teasing. What we really had our hearts set on was some root beer, some Dad's Old Fashioned Root Beer, the one in the brown bottle. Did she happen to have any root beer around? She certainly did not. Root beer was even worse than soda pop.

Part of the routine was to have several bottles of root beer with us, wrapped up in one of our dirty T-shirts. And if we didn't, it was no big deal to jump on our bikes and fly down to Chernikoff's grocery store or Old Man

Pierce's drugstore on Independence Avenue and buy a bottle or two.

"How about a root beer, Grandma, this one's cold."

No.

"Why not, Grandma?"

"Because it's a sin to drink beer."

"No, it isn't beer, it's pop. See, right here on the bottle, you can read for yourself that it's just *root* beer, not beer." We made our case, trying desperately to stifle a giggling fit.

But if it wasn't "beer," she wanted to know, why did they call it beer?

"No, not beer, *root* beer!" But my joshing and sometimes elaborate, and made-up, explanations failed to budge her a half an inch. She would not be drinking any root beer, thank you. She'd not drink beer of any sort. On this, as on all matters of principle, of faith, of truth, she was unmovable. Compared to Grandma, the Rock of Gibraltar was a pebble to be flung by the smallest David on earth.

"Come on, Grandma, it's not really beer. Here, watch me, I'm going to take a big drink."

Occasionally, one of us would take gulps and start to stagger about and sometimes fall down. "You see, he's drunk," Grandma announced each time, playing her role to perfection. But don't let that lilt in her voice or that twinkle in her eye deceive you. She also spoke in a voice of steel that said, "I'm still right." She greatly enjoyed the bantering, but she was not going to take a drink of that beer. Nor was she going to resist getting in the last word.

We were to remember what the Bible said: "Shun the very appearance of evil." The Good Book doesn't say shun evil. Oh no, nothing that easy. It says, "Shun the very appearance of evil." Now she had us, and there would be no escaping the full nelson of her superior logic. "That root beer has the *appearance* of evil. And I'm not about to drink it. And neither should you!" Shun the appearance of evil.

Part of the fun in those days of innocence was to concede the point grandly. And then announce with a flourish that we would go her one better. We would even shun people, no matter who they were, who had the appearance of evil. "From now on, Grandma, lips that touch root beer will never touch mine."

"Me, too, Grandma," Edwin Cavender or Pete Strange, Mr. Jim's grandson, would chime in. "Gimme that bottle. It's gotta be shunned because it has the appearance of evil. I'm not only going to shun it, I'm going to get rid of it right now. I'm going to pour it out. And throw that bottle in the trash where it belongs!" Thunderous applause roared out from the fresh converts to Grandma Gilbert's triumphant teachings.

"Watch me, Grandma, I'm going to pour it out, pour it out on the street, not the grass. I don't want the grass to get drunk. Or the worms. Or the birds that eat the worms!"

Grandma beamed. She radiated righteousness. She was a conquering hero, a theologian with disciples. Onward, Christian soldiers. In time, we might backslide. But we might take hold of ourselves by remembering her words. And for now, well, beer was being poured into the streets where it would run into the gutters, just where it belonged. And who knows, maybe our conversions would stick. You never know.

Grandma Gilbert knew we were joking, helping her to while away the day, and she loved it all, because she loved us. But down deep, she wasn't joking, and everybody knew it. I certainly did. She meant exactly what she said. "Shun the very appearance of evil."

Some small voice warned me that Grandma was right. Now and then that tiny voice—is it mine or is that you, Grandma?—tugs at my heart and grabs my ear and whispers, "Don't just shun evil, shun the very appearance of evil." But it was asking an awful lot of a gangling adolescent to heed the warnings of that small, stern voice, particularly one who had already fallen for some of the allures of Sodom and Gomorrah.

4

Buck

B uck stands in the shadows. He seldom speaks, usually letting others talk. Word was, he wasn't given to talking much anyway, particularly to my father or to my grandmother, Minnie Workman Clayton. But he could be downright garrulous when his buddies showed up or after he got a drink or two in him.

Buck Clayton died several years before I was born. But everyone who knew him told stories about him, usually to drive home a point about drink or what a handsome devil he was. How Minnie Bell Workman, a short woman with a big Missouri farm girl's face, a face to fit her name, ever snared him was a big question, one that had no answer, at least that anyone could say with any certainty.

She was plain. And miserly. Not spending a dime made her day, and gave her something to cackle about. He, though, was rakishly handsome, his face boyish and unlined when he was young. At some point when he was a young man he put on his gray Sunday-go-to-meeting suit and took himself to Kansas City and had his picture taken with his hat tilted jauntily to the back. He liked

Grandma Clayton: not spending a dime made her day.

what he saw so much he bought the whole package: a large picture and a stylish oval frame with curved glass.

When he was in such a rare good mood he liked to have a good time. He didn't complain about spending money on whiskey. Cigarettes and cigars he rated one of life's pleasures—and he didn't care what the Gilberts or anyone else at the Church of Christ thought. He drank until he got good and tight. Then the world brightened and he could be a regular cutup. Around his drinking buddies, that is.

But mostly he was cold. And silent. No one ever knew exactly what he was thinking, except of course when he

Buck took himself
to Kansas City
and had his
picture taken.

went "up town" in Wakenda and fell in with those loafers who should have been seeing to their crops, but who preferred to smoke roll-your-own cigarettes and gab.

Ordinarily, Buck didn't have much to say. But he could get wound up about something he had read in the *Kansas City Star*. Politics mainly. He was a hard-headed Republican, seemed to care about that sort of thing. That's why, folks said, he bothered with that Kansas City paper. The *Star* was rock-ribbed Republican. If Buck was of a mind to, he could talk your leg off and back it up with facts. People reckoned that he knew what he was talking about since no one else read much of anything except the Carroll County *Democrat*. Taking the *Star* was Buck's idea. "Goodness knows your grandmother wouldn't have spent a nickel on any newspaper," Mom said.

But William Valentine Clayton, known to any and all of his neighbors and kinfolk as "Buck," put his foot down. He would have his newspaper, and have it delivered by mail. Buck didn't give a hoot what it cost and didn't want to hear anything more about it. The fact that few if any of the yokels in town subscribed to the paper proved nothing except that they were happy in their ignorance. That was Buck all over.

But catch Buck during the week when he was sober or when he had fallen back into his typical black mood, well, then he could be about as cold as a man can get. Folks said you could walk into his farmhouse two miles outside Wakenda and he'd be sitting in the front room by the heat stove. He'd be sitting reading his newspaper or a magazine, and like as not he wouldn't even look up, let alone speak, until he was good and ready. Sometimes he never got ready. You might go to his house on a rainy day or when it was too cold to do anything but the absolutely necessary chores and he would just be sitting staring at the stove. Or he'd be dozing, or pretending to, so that he didn't have to look at you. "And acknowledge your presence," Mom volunteered.

"I agree! I don't think he cared whether you lived or died," Mom's cousins liked to say. Buck looked neither to the right nor to the left when you entered the room. "Howdy Buck" might get you a cold stare or nothing at all. Then you knew he was in one of those dark moods. Sometimes he stayed that way for days. "Probably drinking," said Mom.

At first, when they had just set up housekeeping back

at the turn of the century, Minnie would try to humor him and break through that awful wall of brooding silence. But it seldom worked.

"What do you suppose he was thinking about?" I asked.

"I have no idea," Dad replied. "Don't ask me about him." On other occasions the same question got an answer, of sorts. "He hated farming. He knew he was wasting his life and had never amounted to anything. And never would."

"Well, I'll tell you about him," my mother never hesitated to say whenever Dad or some of the cousins sitting on the front porch mentioned his name or wondered for the one-millionth time about his death. "He was just plain mean, and a slave to drink. I ain't saying he didn't hate farming. But he was mainly mean. Of course, Grandma Clayton was just the same."

The man was mean, Mom enjoyed pronouncing. "That's just the way your grandfather was. Mean!" Dad would take a long drag on his cigarette, flicking the ashes over the porch banister. He too could turn into an iceberg of silent anger.

"I've said it before but I'll say it again. Your Grandfather Clayton was as independent as a hog on ice." When quizzed about how independent a hog on ice could be, and what did that mean about my grandfather, Mom said, "He did only what he wanted to do. Nothing else. If he wanted to skip church, he did. If he wanted to drink, he did. If he didn't want to talk, he didn't."

More ashes flew over the banister. "There was no changing him, though Lord knows Grandma Clayton tried." It wasn't good manners that prompted Mom to refer to Dad's parents by their last name, but a long-held, smoldering grievance against Buck and particularly Minnie Clayton for never having "treated me right. Never made me feel like a daughter-in-law."

Soon after Mom and Dad were married in 1924 and had set up housekeeping on a farm near Buck and Minnie's place, Grandma Clayton had Buck go to Carrollton and buy one new chair—for their son.

"Why, what in the world did she think I was going to sit on?" Mom blurted out each time the story was told.

"Oh, you never understood her," Dad replied. "You never understood her fear of spending money. Anyway, you exaggerate."

"Do I?" Eyes snapping now, Mom reminded everyone that when they were back on the farm in those first days of marriage both of them would be working in the fields and Grandma Clayton would show up with a sack lunch. "One sack lunch, you understand! It was for your dad. What did she think I was going to eat? I worked as hard as any man. I tell you she was mean, mean clear through, mean as he was in her own way."

She was bound to say it: "Grandma Clayton wasn't ever going to get that man changed. She'd met her match in William Valentine Clayton. He was set in his ways and wasn't about to change. No sir!"

"Did he ever talk to you, Mom?"

"Oh, once in a great while. He didn't care about what I might have to say. And he only talked about what he wanted to talk about, something he had read in the *Star* or somewhere else."

He was no good for gossip or church news. "He wouldn't go to church, except now and then. And, likely as not, he'd bolt right for the door the moment services ended, speak to no one, and head home as fast as his team of horses would carry him." But Mom wasn't finished; she hadn't said her piece. Just thinking of Buck's ornery ways got her dander up. "The menfolk liked to stand and talk awhile after church. Be sociable. But not your grandfather. Oh, no. He probably went up town to sneak a drink with some of those no-accounts hanging around Boss Womack's place."

"Now, you don't know everything about him," Dad erupted. Talk about his father made him squirm. He intended to hush my mother and squash the whole discussion. If that didn't work, he got up and hurried to the basement or for the car and often wouldn't return for hours. If quizzed about where he'd been so long, he usually said blankly, "The hardware store."

"Listen," Mom invariably said in a voice that betrayed her love of a good fight that just might let her settle the score after all these years. "You know, I've always blamed your mother for a lot that was wrong with him. She nagged him something awful. You can't deny that. Anyway, as you know, I've always said there was something likable about your father." Just what was likable about that independent hog on ice, she never spelled out. She cared mainly about getting her licks in about Grandma Clayton.

Nobody seemed to know where William Valentine got that nickname, Buck. Maybe he had been a hellion in his youth, a real buckaroo not to be tamed by the fields of corn or the demands of a miserly wife and two children, or of life in the slow lane that led into and out of tiny Wakenda, the place of Great Mystery.

"Going up town," or "going into town," was one of the few pleasures of those days, especially for fellows like Buck. "Town" at least boasted a grocery store, a post office, an imposing Methodist church (the upscale rival to the Church of Christ), a gasoline station, a feed store where you could also buy farm tools, "Boss" Womack's blacksmith shop, a restaurant, a grain elevator, and a railway depot. One of the joys of Wakenda was to watch the Santa Fe Railroad passenger and freight trains roll into town, occasionally stopping just long enough to drop off or take on passengers. Visitors were prized. They had bits and pieces of news of the outside world.

In the 1936 presidential campaign, in the heart of the Depression when farmers found it cheaper to burn the corn crop for heat than to haul it to Carrollton to sell, Franklin Delano Roosevelt's Victory train stopped for a few minutes. The president waved majestically to an admiring crowd of farmers in their bib overalls and farmwives in plain cotton dresses, some of them made from the cloth of feed bags.

Buck liked going up town as well as the next person, and probably a lot more than most. Sometimes he didn't mind if his only son, Roy Roosevelt, tagged along with him, as long as he didn't make a fuss. (Roy Roosevelt, born in February 1902, was named for Buck's hero Teddy, who had been sworn into office just months earlier following the assassination of William McKinley.) Buck usually ran into someone who would offer him a snort of whiskey or some gossip.

"Boss" Womack, the town blacksmith and self-appointed dispenser of news, was Wakenda's town crier. "Did you hear the news?" Boss boomed out to any and all who entered his hot, dirty shop. On this particular day Boss had big news and he was busting to tell about it.

"Say, Buck, did you hear the big news?" Boss Womack asked excitedly. It was April 16, 1912, late Tuesday afternoon, and Buck had indeed read the news. That's why, coming in early from the fields, he had hurried up town with the boy, Roy Roosevelt, trailing after him.

"No, Boss, what big news?" Buck wasn't about to cheat Boss Womack out of his big announcement. "What happened?"

"What happened? I'm fixin' to tell you what happened! Just listen to this. A big boat went down!"

"Really?" Buck replied, enjoying the fun. "No foolin'? Tell me about it."

"Well, a really big boat went down," Boss boomed out. He'd heard tell that a lot of people had drowned, "Why, no telling how many had drowned."

"You don't say," Buck said. "Any idea what boat?"

"Are you kidding? That big boat was the *Panic*."

"Whereabouts?" said Buck.

Bewilderment, disbelief clouded Boss's grimy face. If Buck didn't beat all. Not having enough sense to know, or to figure out, where any big boat in those parts would go down.

"Why, up the river," Boss sputtered, gesturing south in the direction of the Missouri River, which meandered a couple of miles away and formed a sort of U around Wakenda. Just where—it might have been back east, around Wellington at that tricky bend in the river—the *Panic* had gone down, Boss couldn't say with any certainty. He was waiting for further information.

On the way home Roy Roosevelt, age ten, pestered Buck to tell him more about that big boat. But Buck merely muttered something about that damned fool and how Boss probably had originally thought that the *Titanic* had gone down somewhere on Wakenda Creek. Reckon not. Not even Boss was that dumb. When they got home Buck picked up his newspaper and handed it to Roy Roosevelt. "Here, you can read all about it. Who knows, you might learn something. Then you can be as smart as Boss Womack."

For greater excitement once warmer weather arrived, Buck hitched up the wagon on Saturday mornings and took off with his family for Carrollton, ten miles away. Carrollton, county seat of Carroll County, had a stately courthouse, a town square, an ice-cream parlor, lots of stores, and, by the 1920s, a movie theater.

For Roy Roosevelt the summers were the best—that's when the circus came to Carrollton and folks from miles around rolled in in their wagons or Model T Fords. Pretty girls showed up, dressed in their best summer dresses. Some of them liked to dance, have a good time, and, when no one was looking, take a sip of beer or whiskey—"but don't you fellows go getting any ideas." Of course, if they were good Church of Christ girls (and Carrollton boasted a stern and steadfast congregation) they didn't dance, or go to the movies, and said, "I certainly don't have to drink and dance to have a good time."

Buck parked Minnie and his young daughter with some of her kinfolk, flipped Roy Roosevelt a quarter, told him he had the run of the town, and took off, not to be seen again until evening, when he usually stumbled back to the wagon drunk. Unfortunately, drink didn't improve his mood when he was around his family or "decent folks." Around them the black dog in him came out and he was meaner than usual.

He wasn't in any mood for a lecture from Minnie. He wasn't in the mood for any talk. He took out his anger (that "meanness") on the horses, driving them hard. Part of the road followed winding Wakenda Creek from Carrollton to Wakenda, and Buck delighted in whipping the horses and steering the wagon wheels as close as possible to the edge of the creek. He wanted danger, and by God he was going to have it. Minnie knew it was pointless to protest. Roy Roosevelt and his kid sister had learned the same thing. Hang on, hope, and pray. But drunk or sober, Buck, bleary-eyed and angry, piloted them home in one piece.

Buck hated Sunday mornings. He had little use for religion, particularly the narrow lanes of belief laid out in the church of his upbringing, the Wakenda Church of Christ. Anyway, Buck announced, if pushed, he was an agnostic. He'd be a mighty big hypocrite going to church, so he'd stay home today. Minnie now and then objected, sometimes vehemently, saying he just might learn something at service, something that would do him good, and help him change his hateful ways. That did it. He was staying home now for sure.

Minnie Clayton wasn't particularly pious, but attending church was one of the few occasions she had to see people and talk some. They didn't "entertain" in those pinched days, except to have a meal now and then with a cousin who happened to drop in or a hired hand who took part of his pay in meals. Depending on his mood, Buck argued his case for not going or just refused to get up from the breakfast table. "You go on, Minnie, and take the boy with you. He can drive the wagon."

Buck hated Monday mornings. He hated farming. It was dreary, humdrum work. When it was time to pick the corn he had Minnie take the reins of the wagon, and he and the boy walked along on either side picking the ears and throwing them into the wagon. If by chance an

Roy Roosevelt,
Buck's Boy.

ear flew over and hit Buck, he yelled, "Damn it boy,
watch where you are throwing that stupid thing." If also
by chance Buck pitched one and hit his son and the boy
said a word, or worse yet, cried, Buck hollered, "Damn
it, keep your eyes open, then you won't get hit."

At the supper table—or at any meal—Buck ate in
silence. When he wanted something, say some fresh biscuits or some jam from the larder or another glass of
milk, he tapped his glass with his knife to get Minnie's
attention. She was to do his bidding. After supper he
took to his chair (by the heat stove in winter) and buried
himself in the *Kansas City Star* or the *Saturday Evening
Post.* He went to bed early, usually saying little to anyone.

What did he dream about? What was bothering him? Was it simply that he hated farming, that he was a failure? Wasn't there something more inside him, down deep, than simple meanness? He never said. He just sat there in silence, finding relief, or momentary joy or oblivion, in the bottom of a bottle.

But not enough joy. There wasn't enough whiskey in the world to fill that dark hole in him, that deep crater of dissatisfaction with his life, with his wife, with everything connected with himself and everyone around him. What had he expected? Had he, perhaps in the flush of boyhood innocence, hoped to sail wondrous seas, gaze on strange shores? If so, what had happened to Buck's polar star? Who was he, anyway? Minnie and the boy who became a young man and married and started farming just outside Wakenda (and despised farming, too) saw only the outer manifestation of Buck's anger and depression.

Roy Roosevelt escaped Buck and Wakenda for several years, beginning in 1916. Buck insisted the boy continue his schooling after finishing the eighth grade. That few other youngsters in Wakenda ever went for more schooling meant not a hill of beans to Buck. They could stay ignorant. But the boy, Buck told Minnie, was going on to high school.

For more than Wakenda's one-room grade-school education, Carrollton's high school was the answer. The boy could board with some of Buck's tight-fisted family. They could use the money. And so Roy Roosevelt, unknowingly living out some of Buck's unfulfilled desires, went on in school. The boarder didn't exactly hate every minute of it, but he felt lonely and hungry and out of place most of the time.

America was in the Great War by April 1917. Young boys from Wakenda and Carrollton, itching to escape those lonely cornfields, those dusty roads, enlisted and took off. The next year, in 1918, Roy Roosevelt, age sixteen, quit school, swore to the recruiter that he was eighteen, and left to join the navy.

He joined to escape and to see the world, doubtless to Buck's envy. By the time Roy Roosevelt was in uniform and aboard ship in December 1918 the war was over. But the young sailor had his term to fulfill. He was a proud swabbie, all decked out in white, on the massive battleship the *USS Wyoming*. The gunboat cruised the waters off Cuba, went through the Panama Canal, did maneuvers off the coast of Chile, and steamed for Hawaii.

At sea and in exotic ports like Honolulu the young farm boy became a man—or at least attained a man's desires. He acquired a taste for travel and women, and enough knowledge of the big world to make him restless to the end of his days. He also developed his own fondness for drink. By the time his term was over, early in the 1920s, he was a real sailor. To prove it, his left arm now sported an impressive tattoo of an American eagle, perched and ready to fly away.

Fly away, Roy Roosevelt! Take off! You've got the wings of youth! Listen just this one time: don't go back to Wakenda. Surely you know full well that you've outgrown that narrow backwater. You'll never be happy there. You hate the place. Why, not once during your three-year stay away did you ever write to anyone. You never so much as sent an "I'm OK" letter home. Standing there in Honolulu gazing at the beach and the elegant pink Royal Hawaiian Hotel, did you even send a postcard to your folks? No, you did not. Listen up, Roy

Roosevelt! Don't go back to Wakenda. You've tasted some of the world's wines, felt some of its women, and sung songs they won't understand, appreciate, or tolerate along the banks of Wakenda Creek. But Roy Roosevelt the sailor can't hear us, even if we scream.

So, he returned to Wakenda with some money in his pocket but without prospects or the courage to do anything other than what the village expected of him. The Boss Womacks of the place wanted to know only were you "over there"? After a while, Roy Roosevelt gave up trying to explain that, no, he hadn't been over there but he had been in the war, just the same. Boss wasn't impressed. But Boss wouldn't know where over there was if it reached up and slapped him in the face.

The young veteran with the bold American eagle tattoo had saved a few dollars from his navy pay, enough to buy himself a brand new Model T Ford. A young buck himself, he drove his new smart tin lizzie around town and up and down the dirt farm roads. In time he leased some acres of good Missouri bottom farmland just around the bend from Minnie and Buck's place.

He even attended the church of his upbringing and promptly started "sparking" Lily Ruth Gilbert, six years his junior, who didn't think she approved of that tattoo. Ah, but he was a worldly, older man, somewhat dangerous, even. Is that what attracted her?

Whatever it was, she was banking on her powers of persuasion to get Roy Roosevelt straightened out once they were married. She had never seen anything of the world but never missed a service of the Wakenda Church of Christ. She kept the Sabbath holy: Sunday was for church, Bible reading, and prayer. It wasn't for listening to the new contraption called the radio, unless one lis-

Lily Ruth was banking on her powers of persuasion to get Roy Roosevelt straightened out.

tened to the Blackwood Brothers sing hymns. She frowned mightily on drinking, smoking, loafing, or any idleness. She hoped and prayed that someday she would produce a son who would preach the gospel so that all might hear and be saved.

And Buck? He went on farming and drinking and brooding—and told nary a soul about whatever it was that was driving him mad. Age didn't mellow him. He remained gruff and uncommunicative. Somewhere in some distant America, way too far away for many in Wakenda to see, some folks enjoyed the Roaring Twenties, the Jazz Age, but it was a world Buck could only read about in his newspaper and the *Saturday*

Evening Post. Who knows, maybe he read F. Scott Fitzgerald's celebrations of flaming youth, of partying, of living it up, in the pages of his magazine. If he did, it didn't cheer him up. Around Wakenda, farming and life for Buck were depressed—and the Great Depression hadn't even begun yet. Buck trudged on, drinking and staring at the heat stove.

Sometime during the late twenties Buck rigged up a rope in the barn and tried to hang himself. He was probably drunk. Anyway, he bungled the job and ended up injuring his leg or ankle. One family story had it that he actually broke his leg, or maybe it was his foot, and hobbled about doing the chores and tending to his land and refusing to talk about how he came to limp for a season. Was he a failure at everything?

Sometime in the early 1930s, when the Depression laid its cruel hand on Wakenda and times got even worse, Buck began to taunt Minnie in a new way. In the morning, usually on the weekends, as he stood shaving, he liked to sharpen his straightedge razor extra sharp and then hold it to his lathery neck and call out, "Minnie, come in here. I'm fixin' to do it. I'm fixin' to cut my throat. Come on in here and watch!"

Just like that he said it. No whimpering, no crying out for help, but no bragging, either—just a simple statement of intent: I'm fixin' to do it. But he didn't. Still, no one who ever heard him say it (and he didn't reserve his scare tactic for Minnie alone) doubted that Buck, a cruel, hard man who turned his self-loathing into abuse of others, was up to something.

One day in 1932 he went out to the barn, carrying an empty cup. He walked back into the house, went over to the kitchen sink, and, uttering not so much as a peep to

Age didn't mellow him: Buck in 1932, just before he killed himself.

Minnie, who was sitting nearby, put the cup to his lips. He drank deeply of that bitter cup. He staggered a half step backward. Then he slumped to the floor. Minnie jumped from her chair and ran to the writhing body. She saw in a moment that Buck was in agony, his eyes clamped shut.

William Valentine "Buck" Clayton, that handsome devil in the oval-framed photograph, was, at the end, as independent as a hog on ice. He had gulped a cup of strychnine. His insides were on fire; he'd thrown himself into hell. But true to the end to his dreadful code of stony silence, as he lay dying he uttered not a word, not even a sound. He was fifty-four years old.

In time, Minnie Workman Clayton turned the farmhouse and some of the land over to her son and daughter-in-law and bought a house in town. There she lived on alone for another thirty-odd years. After the folks moved to Kansas City, a tenant farmed the land, taking half of the profit the crop brought in, my grandmother pocketing the rest. She lived most of those years on Social Security—wonder what Buck, the Republican, would have thought of that?—and pinched her farm profits as tightly as possible. Loans from Grandma Clayton—whose maiden name was Workman, remember—were pretty hard to come by, and they had to be paid back promptly. With her, there were just no two ways about it, not when it came to money.

In winter, even on the bleakest, coldest days, she sat alone by the stove bundled up in coats and blankets to save on coal. Fate had dealt her a hard hand—first Buck's meanness and then years of loneliness. But she refused to complain, even after my father finally gave up on farming in 1943 and moved his family to Kansas City. There he and Lily Ruth found good-paying jobs first in the defense plants and then at the Ford Motor Company. He drove to Wakenda once or twice a month to visit her, to see how she was getting on.

She was fine. She saw no reason to complain. "You must be doing all right, Roy, driving that shiny new Ford."

As a young boy during those Saturday visits I roamed around Grandma's yard and yearned for a chance to go out to the "old place" where a ghost I never knew had lived and died violently. We went once or twice. Once there, I made a beeline for the barn, hoping to see where Buck had tried to hang himself. Peering through the window into the dilapidated house, I stood and stared at the washbasin where Buck had threatened to slit his throat and where he had finally done the deed in his own way. Like a man. Like a sad, angry man, forever a stranger to me and everyone who ever pretended to know him.

After my grandmother died Dad sold the land and the house in Wakenda, and the place became only a dark memory and, true to its ancient roots, a great mystery.

5

Gods in Pinstripes

My wildest dream came true on April 10, 1951. That day, the fabled New York Yankees with Joe DiMaggio and the rest of the gods in pinstripes came to Kansas City to play ball. It was an exhibition game against the old Boston Braves—not yet the Milwaukee or the Atlanta Braves. Opening Day was just around the corner, and the Yankees and the Braves, now that spring training had concluded, were on their way back north.

A chance to see my heroes in action was too good to be true. But it's Tuesday, and aren't you supposed to be in school? Are you kidding? You can go to school any-time. Here's the deal. Ditch school with a couple of buddies and take the bus to the ballpark, or hitch a ride with some of the older kids who will drive.

I mean, how often are you going to get a chance to see the New York Yankees, the "World Champions"? The Bronx Bombers had knocked off Philadelphia's bally-hooed "Whiz Kids" in the World Series the year before. It had taken my heroes only four games. Each game had been a pitchers' duel, a masterpiece. Raschi, Reynolds,

Lopat, and Ford had outpitched Jim Konstany, Robin Roberts, and the rest of the Phillies' staff. I'd listened to a couple of the games on the radio and seen film highlights of the series over the winter at Macy's Saturday morning Knot Hole Gang program.

So, a little thing like a day of junior high school wouldn't keep me from the game of the year. Some things are worth dying for—which is about what would have happened to me had my folks gotten wind of where I spent the afternoon.

Kansas City had a minor-league ball club in those days, the "Blues," a Triple A team, the "top farm club of the Yankees," said the Thompson Street kids, strutting with pride. The Blues were in the American Association and squared off against the Toledo Mud Hens, the St. Paul Saints, the Indianapolis Indians, and other stalwarts of the future. The Blues were usually pretty good, mainly because the Yankees had a lot of "prospects" who prepped for the bigs by briefly dazzling Kansas City. Every fan in Kansas City had a hero on the Blues, those "can't miss" wonders who would shine someday for the Yankees. I would have bet two piggy banks that Cliff Mapes and Bob Cerv, two power-hitting outfielders, would make it big someday, maybe end up in the Hall of Fame. (Neither did.)

In Kansas City in the early 1950s you either loved or loathed the Yankees. There was no middle ground, not if you were a fan. To me, the Yankees were what FDR, Truman, Walter Reuther, and the UAW were to my father, what Jesus and the Church of Christ were to my mother, what the New Deal was to everyone on Thompson Street, and what Pope Pius and the Catholic Church were to Little Italy.

But die-hard Yankee haters groused that at the tail end of every season, just when the Blues looked like they were going to edge out the Columbus Red Birds or the Minneapolis Millers, the Yanks called up our best players. Those big shots in New York don't care a bit about Kansas City! "The Yankees don't care about the Blues!" Such lamentations were silly, downright sacrilegious. Mr. Jim agreed.

Even some folks on Thompson Street fell for this malarkey. I tried to reason with them calmly, to show them by unassailable baseball logic that the Yankees, being the "major-league team," had every right, even duty, to take our best players as they fended off the pesky Boston Red Sox or the upstart Cleveland Indians with Feller, Garcia, Lemon, and Wynn.

But neither logic nor my adoration for DiMaggio or any of the heirs of Ruth and Gehrig carried the day. Mule-headed people made Yankee hating into a religion. "Break up the Yankees," they cried. Even *Life* magazine got on the bandwagon, but I hated the Yankee haters.

Before the Yankees-Braves game started I made my way down to the first-base dugout. Maybe I'd get lucky and see Joe D. in person, up close, maybe get his autograph. When Mickey Mantle, running in from the outfield, passed within a few feet of me and waved, I joined the chorus chanting, "Mickey, Mickey, Mickey." Was he only nineteen? He looked magnificent. He was magnificent.

Near the dugout Tommy Byrne, the Yankee's erratic southpaw, was warming up. Pop! Pop! His fast ball snapped in the catcher's glove. But why is Ralph Houk, that second-stringer, squatting there catching Byrne's blazing fast balls? Is Houk going to play today? Talk about lousy luck. We'd paid good money. We'd come to see Yogi Berra, not this guy Houk, who never gets to play, and can't hit. Where's Yogi? We want Yogi.

At that moment who should stroll over from the other side but Warren Spahn. The great Warren Spahn. The legendary Warren Spahn of the magnificent windup and high leg kick, master of a wicked curve ball that made opposing batters go weak in the knees. The tall lefty was lean and lanky just like he looked in the photograph I had taped on my bedroom wall. His crooked nose made him look like some great bird of prey. "Spahnny"—wasn't that what his teammates called him? Here he was, "as big as life," as Mom would say.

Just ten or so feet from the railing that separated mere boys and true gods was Spahnny, forever linked in baseball lore with his famous pitching mate, Johnny Sain. We were in luck. Johnny Sain, he of the hard overhand curve ball, a pitch that could bring tears to the eyes of grown men, was scheduled to pitch today. Still, how could the Braves possibly win the pennant with but two pitchers, even great ones? Simple, cried the scribes: "Spahn and Sain, and pray for rain."

Spahnny loped along with a baseball bat in his hand to where Houk was squatting and stepped into an imaginary batter's box. Houk grinned. What's going on here? This "fraternizing," I guess, was allowed in spring games. Anyway, Spahn and Houk and Byrne were in different leagues. But come the "regular season," when the real competition began, things would be different. Believe it.

Spahnny flashed a big grin at his adoring fans, stepped back a few feet, and said his teammates had sent him over to take a peek at Tommy's curve ball. Spahnny stepped forward, took a couple of mighty swings, put the bat on his shoulder, and nodded to Houk that Tommy could throw now.

This was great. Byrne sauntered up to Spahnny, stopped, and explained grandly that he needed a plate if someone was loony enough to stand in against him with a bat in his hand. The Yankee lefty took out an enormous wad of chewing gum and placed it on the ground in front of the catcher. Spahnny's grin was nowhere as big as mine. I told you this was great.

Byrne returned to the mound, looked in for a "sign." The first couple of signs had to be waved off. Byrne was grinning as much as everyone else. He wound and threw pitch after pitch over that wad of gum. Each pitch was belt high; each snapped into Houk's glove, each a perfect strike. Spahnny, grinning, never took his bat off his shoulder. He greeted each pitch with a slow shake of the head and the cry, "Ball, Tommy, way outside." Or "Try again, Tommy. Ball, too high." Or "Too bad, Tommy, way inside." Byrne chuckled.

"Don't crowd the plate on this one," Byrne yelled out after carefully studying and grandly waving off several signs. This was lefty against lefty. Titan against titan. Byrne wound up, kicked his leg as high in the sky as possible in imitation of Spahnny's famous leg kick, and uncorked a big looping American Legion curve ball that headed for Spahn and then looped over the imaginary plate. Spahnny jumped out of the box and fell on his backside roaring with laughter. The fans standing nearby roared too. Some shouted. Others applauded. Some jumped up and down and yelled their fool heads off. This was heaven.

Oh, the game was great, too. Byrne pitched a whale of a game. So did Sain. But the Yankees won, 3–2, with the hometown hero, Cliff Mapes, scoring the winning run in the ninth inning. Earlier Joe DiMaggio had singled and Yogi Berra (thank God, they both played) had two hits. The mighty Sain pitched well, but lost.

But the buzz of the day was Mickey Mantle's future. The nineteen-year-old blond, blue-eyed Apollo from Commerce, Oklahoma, went hitless against Sain, but in running out a couple of ground outs he stunned the crowd. What speed! What grace! He was a blur as he sprinted toward first base or ran down fly balls in the outfield. I know, I know. He had been a shortstop when the Yankees signed him the year before, but he was being groomed to play center field and fill DiMaggio's shoes. "We'll see about that," said Mr. Jim.

The Mick was not proving to be an instant success in the field, but he had hit the cover off the ball all spring, and Casey Stengel bragged about him. He'd learn to play the outfield, I told Mr. Jim.

But danger loomed. We were at war in some place called Korea, and able-bodied young men were needed. Cynical critics (probably bull-headed Yankee haters!) were saying that just because Mantle was a great baseball player, that didn't mean he didn't have to serve his country. DiMaggio and Williams had done their duty during World War II. So had lots of other stars, including Bob Feller and the Cardinals' Stan "the Man" Musial.

Given all that, the kid from Oklahoma was an easy target. But I was hoping against hope that the Mick wouldn't have to go. Surely people understood that he was DiMaggio's heir apparent and needed to get his trips to the plate and learn to catch fly balls. America ought to get its priorities straight! Where in tarnation is Korea, anyway? I prayed that Mickey could escape the draft somehow and then be assigned to the Blues. That's what Mr. Jim said should be done. Give the kid a chance to learn.

The Mick had been classified 4-F. With those wobbly knees he was certainly in no shape to fight anybody. Besides, he'd rather hit baseballs than go shoot at people he didn't even know. Everybody with any brains knew that, including everyone on Mr. Jim's front porch. But Mantle had looked so healthy all spring, and had hit the thunder out of the ball. So the right-thinking draft board back in Oklahoma caved in—said they'd have another look at him. Maybe reconsider his classification.

I crossed all four fingers on each hand to give the Mick luck—and have him fail his physical. Then I might get a chance to see the next DiMaggio play. Casey Stengel was thinking out loud about having the kid start the season with the Blues. If the Mick fails that test, things would be looking pretty good.

Mickey Mantle failed it flat. Again, those aching knees disqualified him. The doctors called it "chronic osteomyelitis."

The Mick started the season with New York but struggled forlornly with the bat. In mid-July, Casey Stengel decided to send Mantle "down to Kansas City." Everybody I knew flocked to Blues Stadium to watch the Kid from Commerce play. At first he was a bust. While he struggled, Bob Cerv, back from the Yankees also, banged home runs left and right.

Then the Mick started hitting. And throwing. And running. He couldn't be stopped. In one game in early August he personally destroyed the Toledo Mud Hens by hitting a single, a double, a triple, and two homers—all in one game!

Soreheads started saying the kid should be tested again

by the draft board. Yankee haters! Don't they know the guy has bum knees! Give him a break. But no. Maj. Gen. Lewis B. Hershey, national director of the Selective Service, wimped out and ordered that Mantle be tested for a third time. Mantle failed, again and again. Thank you, God.

One golden Saturday afternoon I saw the Mick play. The Kid from Commerce, the future Hall of Famer, smacked a ball to the gap in right center. He had a single, maybe a double. But this was Mantle, remember. He ran like the wind, rounding second and heading for third. He made it! He'd turned a single into a triple! Lord Almighty, could the Mick fly.

I loved that summer—still do. I had seen greatness. I had seen perfection. An immortal had walked the earth in Kansas City that summer of 1951. I'm here to tell you God not only walked. He flew. Faster than the wind.

6

Drugstore Cowboys

After all these years, arrows of memory dart back to Pierce's Drug Store. It was a mom-and-pop operation, though few people, believe me, ever thought fondly of grumpy old Mr. Pierce or his brisk wife. They had some grown children, and they may have been tender and loving at home. But once they entered their corner store they were unsmiling tyrants, itching to squeeze every penny possible from the store. Maybe they had friends, maybe there were people who liked them—but no one I knew ever had a kind word to say about either one, particularly Old Man Pierce.

His store was nothing to brag about. In the front stood an old-fashioned soda fountain with seven or eight bar stools with revolving seats. The countertop was black marble, sporting shiny soda faucets, a bright red Coca-Cola dispenser, and everything a soda jerk needed.

Small drinks were a nickel; a dime bought a bag of chips and a small carbonated drink served in a glass marked "Coca-Cola" or in an oval, cone-shaped paper cup that slipped neatly into a metal container. When Mr.

Pierce was filling prescriptions or in a room off to the side, mixing or shaking a can of paint, we sipped our shakes directly from the cold metal containers. When he whirled around the corner and caught us, he growled, "You're disgusting! Don't you have any manners?"

Mr. Pierce usually worked in the back of the store, all the while keeping a sharp eye on his little kingdom. He was a big man, but slightly stooped from years of bending over his pharmacist's bench. His voice was loud and raspy. He had big, bushy eyebrows (John L. Lewis eyebrows) that he rubbed often and feverishly, and never more so than when he was agitated or angry, which was often.

Did he ever smile? I can't remember him doing so. He cackled at his own mean wisecracks, and rubbed his hands together after ringing up a big sale. But his face preferred a scowl. He hated all sports or games of any kind, especially baseball. Naturally! The old sourpuss never joked, except to say something that demeaned someone.

"Hateful," my mother said. "Why, his face would probably crack if he smiled."

His prices weren't cheap. But his was the closest drugstore, conveniently located at the bottom of the hill on the corner of Monroe Street and Independence Avenue next door to Smitty's Barbershop and Frank's Restaurant, and across the street from Mr. Jim's favorite bar. The store was open evenings and extended credit to almost everyone. Oddly, given his legendary greed, he seldom hounded people about paying their bills. So, Old Man Pierce, or that "son-of-a-bitch Pierce," as Mr. Jim called him, got a good bit of the neighborhood business.

He feared losing a cent or having to give away anything. His mania for collecting the minutest amount of sales tax bordered on the comical. Missouri coined its own plastic mills in those days—ten red mills or two green mills made up a penny. Old Man Pierce took a fiendish glee in demanding the tax, down to a single red mill.

No mill, no sale. He exempted no one—the aged, the infirm, the unbalanced. He didn't shrink from forcing little old ladies to walk back out to their husbands waiting in the car—all for a lousy mill. He reveled in making youngsters, short a mill or two, hike back to their homes, whatever the weather. All to get a single mill. Of course, no "drugstore cowboy," his hackneyed expression for us, ever purchased anything without forking over those damned mills. No mill, no sale.

But we knew how to tango. When we bought something for a dime or so, we handed over the silver and a penny; if he delayed for a split second in giving us our change, we reminded him pronto that our penny entitled us to change—some mills. "I know, I know," he replied angrily. Sometimes, to amuse ourselves and really get his goat, we bought something that cost ten cents and paid him a dime and a penny. But before he could say anything, or paw around in his cash register for mills, we'd wave him off, saying, "Keep the change, Mr. Pierce."

Every time we entered, Mr. Pierce grimaced, his face a sour compound of anger and despair. In summer we traipsed in shirtless and stinky, our cutoff blue jeans dirty from a dusty infield. Sitting down, we piled baseball bats, assorted taped baseballs, and oily, smelly baseball gloves beneath our stools, or let our baseball cleats clank on the floor. If we were really eager to rile the old man, we stacked them on an adjacent stool—that always prompted him to bark, "Put that stuff on the floor" or "Next time, leave those gloves and cleats outside!"

In the fall we entered bouncing an old, scuffed basketball or carrying a football that we threatened to toss to one another. On summer days just before we were ready to leave, or about the time we sensed that Mr. Pierce was about to bust a gasket, we'd begin pounding baseballs into our mitts—in unison. Whop, whop, whop! Sauntering out, we tossed baseballs up in the air and caught them effortlessly, and dangerously close to his glass shelves. Or we bounced a basketball hard enough to rattle some of the glasses and metal containers behind the counter. We gave him the heebie-jeebies.

He had to accept us and serve us. We had a little bit of loose change, and money was his god. And he needed our parents' business, so he put up with us and, when alone in the store and forced to man the counter, hurriedly served up Cokes and root-beer floats and demanded his money, mills and all. He hated working the soda fountain, particularly when he had to run around answering the telephone or waiting on his other customers.

"What'll you drugstore cowboys have today?" he barked out. He appeared to be biting his tongue when he spoke to us. And he could give those overgrown eyebrows a going over as we made him wait while searching our pockets to see how much money we had.

We mocked him with good manners, tacking on a pronounced "please" and "thank you, Mr. Pierce." We inquired after the store's business. And Mrs. Pierce, how was she? "And how are you feeling today, Mr. Pierce?"

He was "fine, fine." And "Mrs. Pierce is fine, too. Now would you drugstore cowboys like anything else?" He never learned; that question, intended to scoot us out, always prompted us to say, "Glass of water, please, it's mighty hot out there today." That got his dander up. He hated giving anything away. He was in torment. We loved it.

Tucked away in the back corner were two dimly lit, narrow telephone booths with folding doors for privacy. Whenever two of us would cram ourselves in and close the door, Old Man Pierce would grew enraged. For five cents you could talk for hours to a girl you were trying to work up your courage to ask for a date—or until Mr. Pierce stomped around and growled, "Come on, out, God damn it, your time's up."

From the phone booths it was just a step to the news rack. *Look* and *Life* and *Field and Stream* and *Argosy* were there as well as "confession" magazines for women, though young boys with dirty fingers thumbed through them while old Pierce fumed. That automatic stopwatch in his brain began to tick furiously when anyone loitered at the magazine rack. He only grudgingly allowed adults to linger as they browsed through magazines. He seethed when any loathsome drugstore cowboy picked up a magazine. He began to fidget. Then he glared at us. Soon, he was about to explode, shouting, "Put it back or buy it!" One of our favorite retaliatory tactics was to have one of our buddies go to the soda fountain and divert him momentarily by calling out for service.

We prayed for his telephone to ring. "Pierce's A. I. D. Drug Store," he boomed out when he answered. Frequently he got himself into a lengthy discussion with a disgruntled or hard-of-hearing customer. He was a big wheel in the Associated Interstate Druggists and, for a time, served as the group's president. We congratulated him heartily. Our praise was sincere—as president he had to be away from the store many afternoons, leaving the store in the hands of the equally fierce Mrs. Pierce. Out of earshot we called him "Big Chief President."

Stooped little old ladies or slightly deaf octogenarians with involved questions about their prescriptions could tie up Mr. Pierce for moments of glorious reading. Best of all were the angry customers who harangued him about their bills and his high prices. They just might take their business elsewhere, maybe to the new Katz Drug Store down the avenue. Oh, how he hated hearing anyone even mention Katz, the local, expanding chain of large drugstores that beat his prices and opened on Sundays, Mr. Pierce's one day of rest.

Old Man Pierce didn't know it, but we were actually learning something at his magazine rack. We learned about the evils of crime, and how the cops always got their man. This we gleaned from the *Police Gazette,* with its lurid covers of gangsters and drug addicts and its screaming headlines announcing, "Hitler Alive in Venezuela." We weren't taken in much by the hokum about Hitler. But the gruesome pictures of "dope fiends" with needle-punctured arms we looked at with wide-eyed wonder, and fear.

It was heaven lolling at the counter sipping a Coke or a root-beer float, particularly when Mr. Pierce was in the back of the store and one of our buddies, or a neighborhood girl, was working the counter.

Things were even better when Roy Beaty was behind the counter. He was a tall, gangling, red-headed teenager. Smiling became him. He was always happy, a genuinely nice guy. He even had a soft spot in his heart for Mr. Pierce. Such was Roy's amiability that he smiled broadly every time one of us remarked, "Roy, I'd rather be dead, than red on the head." That our adult leaders prattled on about "better dead than red" meant nothing to us, even if we had paid any attention.

Roy was honest and trustworthy. That Mr. Pierce knew. Maybe that's why Roy could work up some sympathy for the old man. But being forced to wait on your best friends—who were definitely not moral—well, that was altogether too great a challenge, even for Roy.

To the left of the bright red Coca-Cola dispenser on the counter sat a large jug of orange concentrate. If we ordered our Coke or cherry phosphate in one of Mr. Pierce's cone-shaped paper containers we could, when our cup was empty, merely reach around with one hand and hold the empty cup under the spigot of the inviting jug. The other hand could then turn the handle and dispense some concentrate. Then all we had to do was hand our cup to Roy and request "a drink of water, please." The scheme was foolproof. The Coca-Cola container blocked Mr. Pierce's view when he was away from the counter. No matter how diligently he spied on us from the back, he couldn't detect our theft, especially if two or three of us sat on the stools to the right.

The inexorable downward flow of concentrate brought a rare smile to Mr. Pierce's face. During our season of crime, he was supremely happy. Goody. Scrooge rubbed his hands gleefully, toting up his profits. He was overheard several times crowing to Smitty, the barber next door, about installing the orange concentrate. Our deception, his ignorance, his greed, made those stolen orange drinks taste like golden nectar. Did we ever feel guilty? No. We reminded each other that our legal consumption of sacks of potato chips and peanuts had also leapt up since we learned how to swipe the orange drink. We were, we reasoned, doing him a service by stealing from him.

One day we were sitting at the counter leisurely drinking our Cokes and eating chips and behaving ourselves, though we had dumped dusty baseball gear on the floor. He stood at the cash register glowering at us. What was new about that? But we were not making any disturbance and, with him standing close by, we weren't even stealing anything.

His face got redder and redder. He approached the counter, grabbed a rag, and started scrubbing the counter feverishly. "Will that be all?" he barked out.

"Glass of water, please, Mr. Pierce," I replied.

"Nope," he shouted, "not today. Out, get out! And don't come back."

We should have left well enough alone and picked up our stuff and vamoosed. But we didn't.

"Oh come on, Mr. Pierce," I said as I arose from my stool, "it's hot today, show a little good sportsmanship."

Bang. The old boy blew a gasket. "Good sportsmanship, good sportsmanship," he sputtered, his eyes blazing. "Was it good sportsmanship when you stole my orange concentrate! Was it? Was it?" He was so angry that all he could do was shout, "Good sportsmanship, good sportsmanship. You good-for-nothing bastards stole my orange concentrate!"

We grabbed up our things and, tripping over each other, scurried for the door. As we left we glanced backward to notice that he had slumped down on one of the stools, putting his head on the counter. For a brief second we actually felt sorry for him.

We stayed away for quite a while after that. We were all a little afraid that he would call the cops. Or call our folks. He didn't. When we started drifting back in—not in groups, but singly—to pick up medicine or packages for our parents or neighbors, he made not the slightest mention of our crime. He never said another word about it. In time we started coming back in groups, but it was never quite the same again. Someone noticed that he had removed the jug of orange concentrate.

Years later, some time after I had confounded Mr. Pierce by becoming a teacher, I returned to visit my folks. I made my way to several of my old haunts, including Lykins Park, but each sent unsettling waves of nostalgia rolling over me. Best to sit on the folks' front porch and read. Lykins was the past; I resolved to think only of the future. It was sad looking over at Mr. Jim's empty chair and knowing I'd never see him or Mrs. Strange again. She had moved to Gary, Indiana, to live with Pete and his family after Mr. Jim died.

Old Man Pierce I could do without. But my mother wanted me to go see him. She'd been bragging about me, telling him that I was a teacher, a college teacher, of all things, down South, in Tennessee. "Can you believe it," she announced to him proudly, but not quite innocently—she knew the anguish her words would cause in "that hateful man." Old Pierce had considerable trouble believing it, hated believing it, but he'd heard the story of my leaping tall buildings too often from my churchgoing mother to doubt it.

When I balked at going down to the drugstore she said she'd go with me. No thanks. I hated to cheat her out of her moment of glory, but if I had to see the old buzzard I'd face him alone. Long gone now was any of the joy I'd felt when I knew that my mere presence would make the old man miserable. Mom had her doctor telephone her prescription in. I could walk down and pick it up. Okay.

When I entered he looked up, nodding reluctantly. He had aged. He was stooped now. His hair was grayer, but those eyebrows were still lethal weapons. He looked up again, cleared his throat, and mumbled, "I'll be with you in a minute." He was still the old master of venom. I should have known he'd make me wait. Memories, sweet and bitter, rolled over me as I scanned the soda fountain, the magazine rack, the telephone booths. Memories of pennies and mills, red ones and green ones, and orange concentrate jangled in my head.

He gazed out at me through the small opening in front of his pharmacist's table and said he didn't quite have my mother's medicine ready yet, but it would be only a few more seconds—and I could be on my way. "You're probably in a hurry to get somewhere." The old guy still had it; that last stiletto pierced my ribs.

But I was prepared for him. I had made sure that I had three or four pennies in my pocket—for the tax. I would have given a small fortune for a handful of those now long gone mills. How sweet it would feel—counting out just the right number. No mill, no sale.

I was ready to do battle. But his backhanded comment about my "hurry to get somewhere" caught me off guard for a second. Round one went to him. I bounced back from the ropes and said, casually, "Take your time, Mr. Pierce." I effected a slight southern drawl. "You just take your time. I've got lots of time."

"So you're a college teacher now, are you, somewhere down South," he said to me as he handed me the medicine. He sounded as disinterested as a stranger on a bus.

"Yeah," I drawled. (That southern drawl would knock

him back a step.) "It's a job."

He knew I was a lazy bastard and that teaching wasn't real work. Still, calling it a job would nick his lip a bit. I was beginning to enjoy our sparring. I was dancing around him, and hadn't even worked up a sweat. This was getting to be fun, just like the old days. Come on, old man, give me your best shot, maybe remind me of the principles of good sportsmanship.

"Teach a lot of niggers, I guess," the old man asserted slyly, rubbing his chin. His contorted faint smile revealed he hadn't been nicked or wobbled at all by anything I'd said. His raspy voice was a master pharmacist's compound of glee and spite. Maybe he spoke out of ignorance; maybe he thought all southern colleges had large numbers of black students. No, he knew what he was doing. He was finally, after all these years, exacting his pound of flesh.

In that dazed second or two after he spoke I remembered his virulent prejudices, his hatred of blacks, in particular. "We don't serve any niggers in here," he had boasted in years back. Only a handful of blacks lived in Northeast, and few ever came on Independence Avenue or into his store. But that hadn't tempered old Pierce.

"Teach a lot of niggers, heah?" I only dimly heard the question repeated. My mind had slammed backward in time to a scorching day in July or August, sometime around 1952 or 1953. Two old black men, probably in their sixties, had come into the store. They worked for the city and were repairing the street in front of Mr. Pierce's store. They dripped with sweat. Their shoulders sagged with fatigue. Hot, tired, they shuffled to the counter. They didn't sit down. They knew the rules, knew that blacks weren't allowed to sit at the counter.

Deference marked their every gesture. But being strangers to the neighborhood, they didn't know the full harshness of Old Man Pierce's rule. They waited silently for someone to ask what they wanted.

My eyes darted from the old black men to Roy, behind the counter, his head bowed, his eyes lowered to a spot on the shiny counter. He rubbed that spot vigorously. Roy reddened with embarrassment. What should he do? Mr. Pierce was away from the store.

In the back, Marvin Shaeffer, Old Man Pierce's elderly, timid evening pharmacist, was filling prescriptions, his head bent over his work. A wee man, Mr. Shaeffer had to perch on a high stool to see out into the store. Silence. No one spoke. The only sound was the agreeable voice of Larry Ray, announcing a Blues game.

Roy looked up, glanced nervously at the men, excused himself, and went to the back of the store. He asked Mr. Shaeffer, who greeted any unpleasantness with a nervous cough, what he should do. Little Mr. Shaeffer listened carefully, then climbed down from his stool, cleared his throat, and walked slowly to the front of the store.

He removed his glasses, rubbed his eyes. He meekly mumbled that he was sorry, but you see Mr. Pierce has his rules. All he could do was offer them a couple of cups of water. "But now you can't drink that in here. You'll have to go outside." Silence. Eyes, faces, black and white, looked down as Mr. Shaeffer turned with his head bowed down and retreated to his workbench. Roy filled two of the largest containers he could find; he asked the men if they wanted ice. They nodded yes. They trudged out. Neither had spoken a word.

"Teach a lot of niggers, do you?" How many times had he stabbed me—two, three, four?

"Yes," I answered, after what must have been an eternity of confusion. No pretend southern drawl now. I had to swallow hard to speak. "Yes," I said again, this time slowly.

I lied. The little mountain college where I taught had only a handful of black students. I had only one or two in my classes. Why did I lie? Had I stooped to his level of meanness? I knew my false answer would leave him with a mixture of torment (a white Kansas City boy, even one he loathed, teaching blacks) and malicious pleasure—he'd known I would come to no good. So intense was my hatred of him that I squeezed some small solace from my lying answer.

Whatever my fathomless reasons, I lied and turned woodenly away, my mouth tasting of cotton. I passed the counter where orange drinks had once seemed sweeter than life itself and where piles of baseball mitts and dusty cleats had rested languidly and driven Old Man Pierce mad. Floundering in a ocean of memories and confused, angry feelings, I walked back to what had once been home. I hadn't even remembered to say, "Thank you, Mr. Pierce"—a breach of etiquette he probably savored for the rest of the day.

Some time later my mother telephoned to report that Mr. Pierce had "passed away." I couldn't think of anything to say about him. She didn't say anything else about him, only that he'd "been poorly for some time." In some unfathomable way I felt that a part of me, a small piece of my past, had died, too.

7

Frank's Filthy Restaurant

F rank had shot a man. A man on a bus had questioned Frank's finely tuned sense of Italian honor. The fool had insulted Frank right there in broad daylight and in front of the other passengers! Frank had pulled out a pistol and shot the man on the spot, wounding him, perhaps killing him. He carried the gun in his suit coat pocket. Many people swore they had seen it once.

Frank laughed a lot and was usually in good spirits, though he was not a man of many words, and he spoke in broken English with a heavy accent that honored his birth in the old country. Just when he came to America I never knew. His voice, punctuated with exclamations such as "I no like you, you bastard," yelled at customers as he ran them out of his restaurant, or frequent shouts of "whadda you think I am, stupeedo," made him sound like he had just stepped off the boat.

Our Frank was short, compact, and of indeterminate late middle age by the early 1950s when I joined other neighborhood kids and began hanging out in his small, dingy restaurant two doors down from Pierce's Drug Store. Pierce, of course, hated him, but he was careful about voicing his venom. Frank wasn't big, but something about that squat little man said don't fool around with me.

He was our mystery man. Had he really killed someone? People said so. That was the word on Thompson Street and up and down Independence Avenue. Had Frank, lord and master of a greasy spoon—which Mom always called that "filthy restaurant"—really shot someone? We hoped so. Mr. Jim believed it. As always, that was good enough for me—that and a very noticeable round dent in the shiny sheet metal directly behind Frank's grill.

That dent must have been made by a small slug. What else? The bullet, we repeated to each other breathlessly, had whistled by Frank's ear. Frank, so the delicious rumor went, had gotten into a shouting match with a drunken customer who had surprised him by yanking out a gun and firing wildly at Frank's head. He bolted for the door—and (wisely) never showed his face around Frank's Filthy Restaurant again. Don't mess with Frank; everybody knew that.

Occasionally a drunk—staggering in from one of the three nearby taverns and hoping to sober up on gulps of Frank's midnight-black coffee and one of his greasy tenderloin sandwiches—would steady himself and blurt out, "Frank, tell me the truth, God damn it! Did you kill somebody?"

"Yeah, Frank, is that true," I chimed in many times.

Frank usually declined to answer. Sometimes he shrugged his shoulders and slowly shook his head. Did we think he was "stupeedo," or "mafioso"? That was the end of it, and drunks or small boys who continued pestering him were told, angrily, "You shut up, or you get out."

"You think if I kill a man I be sittin' here now," he replied if he was in a good mood or if the question was obviously banter. "I tell you where I'd be. I'd be in a bigga jail. That's where I'd be. Or back in the old country, in Sicily."

That Frank was from Sicily and had a wife was about all we ever knew about him. Every midmorning, seven days a week, "Mrs. Frank" (if I ever knew their last name it's now long forgotten) stepped off the bus at the stop right outside the Monroe Inn, across the street from Pierce's Drug Store, and made her way to their restaurant. She aired the place out, wiped down the counter and the tables, and got ready for the modest lunch business.

She was solemn, unsmiling. She seldom spoke. She seemed to have no personality, no identity other than being Frank's wife. Gray sadness enveloped her. Weariness weighed heavily upon her face. An unspeaking resignation clung to her as tenaciously as the film of grimy dust hugged the walls and ceiling of the restaurant. When I think of her now I remember sad eyes, looking neither right nor left, but only to the job at hand. She seems always to be wearing a brown or gray sweater, with a scarf on her head tied at the neck. I think she was a devout Catholic who never missed Mass.

Around 3:30 every afternoon, day in and day out, rain or shine, Frank arrived by bus to take his wife's place. In season and out, Frank arrived in a heavy, old-fashioned, dark double-breasted wool suit, with a white shirt and wide necktie, and a black fedora perched atop his thick, wavy hair. He looked dapper in an old-timey way, though as the years wore on and his hair turned gray he looked more and more out of date. As soon as he entered the restaurant he took off his coat (and his vest on summer's hottest days), loosened his tie, put on a white apron, sat down behind the counter, and started reading the newspaper.

It was a dimly lit, one-room, store-front restaurant; it was always grungy. Mom was right, it was filthy. It had a lunch counter, five or six stools, two or three tables and chairs, a jukebox, and two pinball machines against the back wall. You could order anything you wanted provided you wanted one of two or three sandwiches. You could also have some french fries or a bag of potato chips and a soft drink or simmering ink-black coffee. Specialties of the house were hot dogs, hamburgers, and tenderloins, the latter two served with mustard, pickles, and a dangerous slice of onion.

Frank kept two pots hot—one half-filled with grease (for the tenderloins and french fries) and the other filled with water for hot dogs. He wasn't overly conscientious about scraping down the grill, thinking, perhaps correctly, that the grease gave the hamburgers extra flavor. An odor of stale grease assaulted you the moment you walked in, but after a few minutes you were at ease. For the rest of the day your clothes fired off bazooka blasts at the world. It was no secret where you had been hanging out.

My mother's nose was easily offended by my noxious odor after a session at Frank's. She hated the place—in there one could only be "up to no good, and sure to get in trouble." She loathed pinball machines! They deeply offended her religion and her thrifty nature. Somehow, she got it into her head that playing pinball was a form of gambling. My repeated assertions that I didn't put any of *my* nickels in—a fat lie—and that I only played games won by my friends convinced her all the more that Frank's Filthy Restaurant was as corrupting of boys as the Monroe Inn was of adults.

Nothing could ruin a challenging game of pinball quicker than having my mother stick her head in Frank's place and screech, "You come out of there this very minute." Since we played the machines with our backs to the front window, my mother could sneak up on me and catch me "gambling." "How many times have I told you to stay out of that filthy place?"

Like Pierce's Drug Store, Frank's place had an exquisite charm. It was our place, absolutely perfect for lolling away a rainy day. For a nickel in Frank's jukebox you could hear Patsy Cline croon "Blue Moon of Kentucky," or Frankie Laine holler "Mule Train," or do your part to help usher America into the age of rock 'n' roll by selecting Bill Haley and the Comets' "Rock around the Clock."

A quarter allowed you to confess with the Platters that you were "The Great Pretender," or glide along with the Mills Brothers' "Glow Worm," or whoop it up with Little Richard's extolling of "Long Tall Sally," or wonder with Patti Page, "How Much Is that Doggie in the Window," or belt out "Jailhouse Rock" with Elvis. Or anything by Elvis. Frank didn't mind if you sang along, as long as you kept it down to a low roar. A nickel had power in those days. A quarter was an atomic bomb.

Got a quarter? That will get you a bottle of pop, a sack of chips, two games of pinball (more if you're lucky and rack up some wins and my mother isn't patrolling Independence Avenue), and three and a half minutes of

Pat Boone crooning "Love Letters in the Sand." Too much white bread? You're right: that Pat Boone would gag a maggot!

Night after night, Frank sat reading the *Kansas City Star*. He bestirred himself only to swat a fly or to flip a hamburger on the grill. Want a bottle of pop? "You get it yourself!" Frank was the world's slowest reader. He must have memorized the entire paper. Or maybe he just stared at the photographs and illustrations. I never heard him mention anything he read. Sometimes I caught myself wondering whether he even knew how to read. I kept such thoughts to myself, of course. Remember: Frank's pistol.

"If I was to eatta this newspaper, would I then know everything?" How many times did he ask me that? Hundreds. Each time, his eyes twinkled.

"I don't think so," I told him every time. "Anyway, you know enough already, Frank."

"I don't know nothin'," he'd say, sometimes menacingly.

I didn't argue with him. Once, out of the blue, he whacked my finger with a sizzling spatula. As I danced around the room in pain, waving my burned hand in the air, he chuckled, saying, "That'll teach you." It did. It taught me to watch my hand when Frank waved that spatula around.

One day a pint-size kid, a stranger to the neighborhood, kept pumping nickels into the pinball machine. What an amateur. Hey, Frank, is that peewee old enough to be playing? He looks underage to me.

"He just have to be big enough to put in his money," Frank scowled.

You are right, Frank. "Gimme a tenderloin, mustard, hold the onions."

I often wondered about him. What kind of life had he lived? Was he happy or sad? But he wasn't the sort to inspire such questions. And he didn't say much about himself. When I asked him, usually just to pass the time, whether he ever thought about going back to Sicily, he always replied, "No," sometimes gruffly. He was a man of secrets. Better leave it like that.

He was great to talk to, providing you didn't need much conversation coming back to you. He nodded agreeably to most things and seemed to have few opinions about anything. He didn't even talk about baseball, though his eyes sparkled every time I asked him—fifty, a hundred times?—who were the only three brothers ever to play in the big leagues at the same time. He loved straightening his shoulders and nodding triumphantly before answering smartly, "Gooda question! But that one, old Frank know. One: Joe DiMaggio! Two: Vince DiMaggio! Three: Dominic DiMaggio!"

Who'd they play for, Frank?

"Some of them teams in the bigga leagues, who do you think, the Blues?"

His conversational gambits, other than "you wanna sandwich" or "bottle of pop," revolved around "how's school" and "what you gonna do when you become a man?" Or "maybe you be president of this whole country someday!"

"Old Frank not doin' too bad," was his standard answer to almost any question about himself. Or "it's cold today," or "nice'a day, today."

He had one joke. No one ever knew when it was coming, but once he started you had to go along with it. Where was that hot spatula? That pistol?

You would walk in, primed for some serious pinball.

"Frank, how about some change? How are you doing today?"

"Not too good today." Watch out, here comes Frank's joke. He began mugging, his face contorting into a crazy quilt of seriousness, a wry grin, squinting eyes, furrowed eyebrows. "Last night I had a terrible dream!"

"Holy moly, Frank. What kind of dream did you have?"

"Nightmare!" Frank shouted, waving his arms. He did his best Pagliacci impersonation, though he struggled to suppress a grin. "I'ma dream I'ma layin' naked on a big, warm beach with a case of beer at my feet, and two beautiful naked ladies layin' on each side." He varied the story, now and then, and replaced the beer with wine, "dago red, the best kind."

"Hey, no argument here, paisano."

Another pause. A sorrowful look lumbered over his face; he rolled his eyes heavenward—actually, toward that greasy ceiling. He shook his head slowly to emphasize the shock he felt from his tormented sleep. This was his listener's cue to say something.

"Hey, Frank, that doesn't sound like no nightmare to me. I'll take that dream every night."

"Yeah, but I'ma wake up," Frank replied with as much mock bewilderment, sorrow, and glee as his face and voice could register. "And they all be gone—beer, beach, naked women. Everything!"

"Jesus, Frank! That's one scary nightmare."

No one in that greasy spoon was to start laughing until Frank jumped up from his chair and burst into laughter. Now, you can smile, laugh out loud if you like, but don't ever let on that you're faking it. Later you can try your hand at consoling him, or assuring him that he is one hell of a storyteller, that you almost believed he had a real nightmare.

The little man in the white apron beamed. Frank surveyed his fiefdom of filth and saw that it was good. His eye fell not on a smelly cell of failure but a stage on which he had, for just a minute, strutted with the best of them. Greatly pleased with himself and his little kingdom, with his friends and his mastery of the glories of storytelling, he sat down and was ready for another go at the evening newspaper.

After a decent interval Frank could be approached for some change for the pinball machine or jukebox. "Frank, here's a dime, gimme a sack of chips and a Coke."

What did old Frank really dream about after he laid his tired head, all that wavy hair, down on the pillow? Beaches, nymphs, beer, and wine? Did nightmares ruin his sleep? Did he dream at all? Maybe he drifted off gently to sleep with visions of the golden days of his youth slithering seductively before his eyes. Maybe he dreamed of the old country. Or about his boyhood. Or about the president of the United States. Do you suppose he ever had nightmares about the man he had shot? Maybe he had shot others, maybe he was a wanted man, a marked "mafioso," back in the old country. We hoped so.

Then again maybe Frank's past, like his present, had been ordinary, humdrum, not all that much different from everybody else's. Is it possible that Frank, that wily devil, had two jokes—one about his terrible dream, the other that everybody thought he had at least once in his life done something exciting, like shoot a man? Whatever it was, I never found out.

8

Big Red

We were sure she had dropped down from heaven. Could she have? One somnolent summer day in 1953 she simply arrived in all of her radiant beauty to grace Thompson Street, to give it a sweet loveliness unknown ever before. She moved in with Mrs. Watkins, a quiet, reclusive, deeply religious woman, and her son, Jim Bell, who lived three or four houses down the block.

Our goddess was a statuesque redhead, with a heavenly figure we'd seen only in the movies, or abundantly displayed on calendars down at Bill Groaner's auto body shop, or in our dreams. Here she was; real, in the flesh, flesh we'd never seen before. She had flaming crimson hair, lots of it; shining hair she wore tied up under a bandanna when she tended the flowers in the front yard or helped Mrs. Watkins clean the windows. In the early evenings, she sat on the front porch wearing sleeveless summer dresses or—better yet, to our roaming, inflamed pubescent minds—the shortest shorts we had ever seen and colorful blouses tied beneath her breasts.

She brushed her hair until its redness glistened, adding extra allure to her face's slight reddish complexion and barely discernible freckles. Hair as long and bountiful as hers, we all agreed as we watched her rapturously, required that she toss her head often as she brushed.

She was a dancer, that much we had been able to pry out of Jim Bell, a bookish, skinny, awkward boy a year or two older than the rest of us. Jim Bell (whose name, James William, had been Missourized into Jim Bell) swore solemnly, repeatedly, that he knew only what his mother had told him: that their visitor was a close friend of his sister's—out in Hollywood—that she was a dancer like Jim Bell's sister, whom we had actually seen on the silver screen.

Brainy Jim Bell was a bookworm. He even liked school—he attended a Jesuit "parochial" academy several miles away. We tried earnestly, in vain, to talk him into being more like us. He was considering the priesthood and didn't like our nosy questions one bit. Our incessant fascination with her was "dirty." He cringed when we called her Big Red; he loathed our boasting about the satisfaction we'd give her if she ever gave us a chance.

We laid odds she was "knocked up." Jim Bell grimaced. Or maybe she'd come to Kansas City because she needed "a place to hide out for a while." That had to be the reason. In those morally prim days even the urchins of Thompson Street knew that unmarried starlets and would-be starlets could be disgraced forever by getting pregnant. If she didn't have "a bun in the oven," or hadn't "swallowed a watermelon seed," she might be "on the lam" from the law or hiding out from some gangster boyfriend. If tight-lipped brainy Jim Bell knew, he wasn't saying. We never found out.

I think we liked not knowing too much about her past. With her gorgeous body and a face more beautiful than any we had ever seen, she was from some exotic land we knew nothing about. She was lithe and slender with long, white legs, dancer's legs, legs that turned slightly pink that summer from the sun. Simply by being there, and being who she was, she transformed drab Thompson Street, briefly, into a place of beauty.

How to describe her? We hadn't a clue. We were reduced to groaning "Big Red, Big Red," as we rolled around uncontrollably in the grass out in the backyard or shagged fly balls down at Lykins Park. We murmured "fantastic," or grandly bestowed our highest accolade, "premium." The merest mention of her name could touch off yelling fits of "Premium, Premium, Premium." She was "built like a brick shithouse wall!"

"Hey, turd, watch your mouth," someone yelled in mock seriousness when anyone profaned Big Red in any manner of speaking or gesturing.

No one, certainly no one we knew, had ever seen anything like this heavenly body we worshiped. Sometimes, while riding lazily along on our worn-out bikes, walking down to Pierce's Drug Store, or riding the bus somewhere, the merest mention of her caused our eyes to glaze over, our minds to go aroaming. Presently, someone would moan while staring off into space, "Big Red, Big Red, Big Red. Wherefore art thou Big Red?"

She could not have been older than her late twenties, we told each other. Maybe in her early thirties. Jim Bell swore he didn't know. Big Red must have had a name, and we must have known it, though it cannot be said that any of us really talked to her. She talked mainly to Mrs. Watkins and about feminine matters we weren't interested in or didn't understand. She stood about five foot five—we never got a chance to measure her, though we daydreamed about it and made lewd comments about "measuring" her with our potent, if unused, male members—and we called her "Big Red" simply because we adored her and could think of no higher praise.

Jim Bell was prudish. But Big Red wasn't. She helped Mrs. Watkins out by mowing the lawn. But, God be praised, she mowed in a bikini, the skimpiest bathing suit anyone had ever seen, or dreamed about. That tiny bikini. Mowing the lawn, Big Red was chapter one in the book of revelation. Hollywood (Sin City) had come to one small part of Kansas City—and confirmed everything my mother thought about it.

That bikini was new, breathtakingly new to Kansas City, or to the tiny patch of it I knew. Folks out in cow country, in the age of Harry and Bess and Ike and Mamie, had seen women wearing two-piece swimsuits, but that little bit of nothing Big Red wore scandalized Thompson Street.

"Why it didn't cover anything," Pearly Cavender said from her front porch directly across the street. Pearly didn't miss much, either. She was glad Mr. Cavender, who as a railroad engineer usually worked the midnight run, had to sleep all day and didn't have to see anything as disgraceful as that woman. Big Red's bikini covered something, but not much, and for that not much we were eternally thankful. Big Red was a scandal.

Her frequent appearances in the front yard—whether in short shorts or in her swimsuit—made it mighty difficult to keep our eyes on the ball in our street games of catch or stickball. Not look, not stare? Are you kidding? Let it rain all night, and let the days be hot and sunny.

Then the grass would grow, and Big Red would mow.

When she pushed Mrs. Watkins's ancient mower around the front yard, grown men in cars drove round and round the block, their cars slowing to a crawl as they approached and passed Big Red. Most just gazed silently out of their car windows in adoration. Some leered. Some further defamed our Lady of True Beauty by blurting out, "Hubba, hubba." Jerks! Some pounded on the sides of their cars and shouted, "Mamma mia." Big jerks! Boy, were they dumb.

Big Red, though, paid them no heed. She made no response. Was she so absorbed in her work that she didn't notice? Or amazingly broad-minded, or tolerant by nature? She never took any notice of the gawkers or the rude comments. On she mowed. She paused now and then for a glass of lemonade or iced tea, then resumed her task.

Did she perspire? Surely real, honest-to-goodness human sweat must have dripped under her arms and between her ample breasts, breathtakingly revealed by that mere blur of a bikini top. But if she perspired like mere mortals, she glistened in the sun, and became even more tantalizingly beautiful.

How much more beautiful we discovered accidentally. A two-rung grape arbor decayed gracefully in Jim Bell's backyard. It was a sturdy, aged, homemade contraption constructed out of steel pipe. The grapes grew wild, and the arbor was badly overgrown—always, by late summer, on the verge of riot. The only pruning it got came from our clowning around on it, picking and eating the grapes and breaking off limbs and leaves.

It had been a grand place to hide during earlier years of playing hide-and-seek. Now it was perfect as a place to sit and munch grapes and chatter endlessly about Mickey Mantle or Whitey Ford or Moose Skowron. On hot days it offered a shady, cool hideaway where one or two or three kids could to do absolutely nothing. Older, adventuresome boys who didn't care that smoking would "cut down on your wind" and ruin forever your chance for glory on the big-league diamond used the quiet, overgrown arbor to sneak a cigarette and practice inhaling or blowing smoke out through their noses. Some of the older Thompson Street romeos boasted that the grape arbor was a great place to romance a girl and "sneak a feel." For the rest of us, the arbor was a hangout, another place to sit and talk sports and theorize about how soft and round unfelt breasts must be. Someday we'd get our chance.

And then not Girl but Woman appeared before our eyes. One night, when several of us were sitting on the bars of the arbor doing nothing, the Watkinses' bathroom light switched on. The window shade was up. It wasn't Jim Bell or his mother who entered the room. It was Big Red. Calmly, slowly, she started taking off her clothes. She began drawing herself a tub of water. We sat in stony silence, breathless silence. No one moved. Was she going to lower the widow shade?

She didn't. It was raised about three or four inches above the windowsill. The bathroom was at the back of the house and, like every room in that one-story bungalow, on the ground floor, with the windowsills just slightly above our eye level. Big Red and the bathroom were partially shielded from the neighbor's house across the alley by the grape arbor, trees and bushes, and a dilapidated garage in the neighbor's backyard.

Hearts pounding, we approached the inviting window. We moved on feet silent enough to make a cat envious. By standing on our tiptoes—and later on a couple of carefully placed bricks—two or three of us could peer in and gaze on heaven. The tub was against the wall by the window. When she lay soaking in the tub she was just inches from our noses—and eyes. We could have reached out and touched her. It was a night of ecstasy.

She appeared to be in no hurry. She read a magazine; she smoked a cigarette. When she got up she was pinker and even more beautiful than we'd thought. Pearly Cavender was wrong: that bikini had covered something: nipples, round, pointed nipples, rounder heavenly breasts. And below? Well, she was Big Red all right, no one need ever doubt that again.

She took her time drying off. There she stood in the tub as she wiped the water off—only a few feet from our wide, admiring eyes. She stepped out, and stood naked before the sink and applied various soaps and lotions to her face. Her back was to us now, but we'd seen paradise, and her pink, round bottom looked even better in the buff than in a bikini. Breathe? Are you kidding? Our lungs were about to burst. Then she flicked off the light and was gone.

The next day, sitting on the curb playing mumbletypeg or throwing a ball against the steps, our minds were not on our game, but on Big Red. Visions of her luxuriant beauty danced before our eyes; she filled our minds as never before. We fantasized about her, rudely, obscenely. She was our Lucky Strike cigarette: "so round, so firm, so fully packed." In our minds her breasts became rounder, bigger, softer, more alluring than ever. "Felt breasts are round, unfelt breasts are rounder"— that I would learn one day. And I knew at once that the poet had it right because I remembered Big Red, and gave thanks.

Each of us took an oath: we would tell no one else. We would go back every night and hope with all our might for that window shade to be up. We resolved not to tell Jim Bell; it would certainly not do any good to ask him to make sure that window shade was up. In the boy was the man who would one day take holy orders.

We went back the next night, several of us. We made our way stealthily, resolutely, to the grape arbor, taking the alley so we didn't have to pass between the houses and perhaps alert neighbors or Big Red that Peeping Toms were on the prowl. We arrived early, just as it was getting dark; better early and wait, than late and miss out. The window shade was up. We had hit pay dirt. We waited as quietly as monks, whispering and keeping our fingers crossed. But no Big Red. Seconds, minutes seemed like an eternity.

Then the bathroom light flicked on. It was Jim Bell. That rat, on leaving he pulled the shade down. The light went off. A few minutes went by. We were giving up hope. Then the light came on. Was it Big Red? Someone started running water in the bathtub. But all we could make out through the shade was a very shadowy female figure. It was Big Red, but all we could see was her magnificent silhouette. Two nights earlier and we would have killed for just that much of a tantalizing glimpse. But now that we had seen all of Big Red we hungered and thirsted not for righteousness, but for clearer sightings of paradise.

We waited around, hoping I suppose, in some stupid way, that the shade would fly up or something would happen. We cursed Jim Bell. Finally we gave up and trudged home, feeling very down in the mouth. Our one moment of good luck had been a fluke of nature, a fleeting moment of ecstasy, a fleeting moment of chance. We'd have to settle for Big Red in her bikini.

We went back the next night. The shade was halfway up. We were in luck. The light switched on. We crept silently to the window. Big Red entered. She brushed her teeth and started the water for her bath. She looked at the window. We froze, convinced that she was looking right into our eyes. She'd tell Mrs. Watkins, who might call the police. Had Big Red seen us? If so, she gave no sign. She merely pulled the shade down. We trudged up the alley brokenhearted again. Paradise lost. Why, we asked soulfully, why?

The next day it rained hard all day. The wind blew. It was chilly. Ball practice was rained out; we couldn't even play stickball or have a game of step ball. The rain continued into the evening. Someone mentioned Big Red. "You win some, you lose some," said a kid from down the street, a kid who hadn't been with us that first night of triumph. One of us who'd seen Big Red through the window had told a friend. He'd been sworn to secrecy, but he'd told someone else. Now all the kids on the block knew about it. But it didn't matter anyway. Obviously, Big Red had just forgotten to pull down the shade that first night.

Several of us diehards went back night after night, hoping for another miracle. And night after night we were disappointed; either the shade was down when we arrived or Jim Bell or Big Red pulled it down on entering the room. We shoved off in despair, muttering that we'd merely gotten lucky that one night, and lightning doesn't strike in the same place twice.

And then one night the shade was all the way up, clear to the top of the window. That was no good. Nobody would stay in a lighted bathroom with nothing whatsoever covering the window. When Big Red walked in she looked up at the shade and reached up to pull it down. But she didn't pull it all the way down; she left it a couple of inches up from the bottom. We had hit a grand-slam home run. We hoped to round the bases slowly.

Everything she did that night she did deliberately, almost teasingly. She unbuttoned her blouse languidly. She seemed to move in slow motion. She stepped out of her shorts in a leisurely fashion. She examined her arms and legs carefully before removing her underwear, which she tossed into the corner. There she was, beautifully naked once again.

She brushed her teeth, washed her face. She seemed blissfully unhurried. Something on her leg, right above the knee, caught her attention. When she bent over to turn on the bathwater her deliciously round breasts dangled wondrously before our eyes. Holy cow: everything was, indeed, "up to date in Kansas City." Big Red was "as round above as she was round below."

She soaked contentedly in her bath, seeming at one point to drift off into sleep. She shampooed her hair and shook her head vigorously, so vigorously her breasts jiggled. When she arose, her body pinker than ever from the hot water, she stood and rubbed the towel over every part of her sumptuous body. Everything was done gracefully, even angelically. In that small bathroom she seemed to be dancing slowly, seductively, alluringly, to some silent but vibrant music only she could hear. What a heavenly body. Tonight she was in no hurry; her movements were like a dancer's, she moved like liquid.

Then she lathered soap in her hands, put one leg on the side of the tub and began applying soap to her leg. She shaved one leg, slowly, deliberately, and then gave the other one equal treatment, always keeping her eyes on her body. When she was done she dried herself off again, slipped on her robe, and started to turn off the light. She paused. She turned and looked at the window. She reached across the tub and pulled the window shade down. The lights went off.

We waited a moment and then scampered off as quietly as possible into the night. Had she seen us? She couldn't have. How could she not have? Had she heard us? There was no way she could not have heard us as we jockeyed for position, squirming and elbowing each other. We were only inches from her, in the still of the night.

From that night on, we were never sure when Big Red would favor us again. We went back almost every night. On most nights she closed the shade or left it closed. Some nights she let us have a brief peek. But she never again repeated her earlier, exquisite, and much appreciated performance.

The moms and pops of Thompson Street would have gone through the ceiling had they ever discovered what Peeping Toms we were. Mrs. Watkins would have been mortified. Mom would have tanned my hide. Dad would have bawled me out, yelling that there were laws against Peeping Toms and that I could end up with a police record that would "follow me to the end of my life, no matter where I went." But surely his heart would not have been in his words.

But a beating was nothing to what Mom and the other mothers, in righteous concert, would have done about

Big Red. They would have gone to Mrs. Watkins and alerted her that she was sheltering a harlot and demanded that the offender be sent packing—now! It would have been self-evident to Thompson Street moms that Big Red was a corrupter of their youth, soiling us forever, planting sinful thoughts in our tender minds. Why, there was no telling what might become of a young boy allowed to see such things, such nudity—that bikini swimsuit was bad enough. It inflamed the imaginations of even grown men, good and true, who were mature enough to say no to temptations of the flesh.

Down deep we knew we would have turned to jelly had she ever even so much as winked at any of us.

And then, without a warning, she was gone. And gone forever from Thompson Street, gone forever from our lives. But never from memory.

9

There Was Always Church

C hurch. Always church. Sunday mornings. Sunday evenings. Wednesday night, too. It wasn't up to *you*, Christian Soldier, to decide whether you wanted to go. Don't go falling for the Devil's tricks. Nothing was more important than services at the Twenty-sixth and Spruce Street Church of Christ. Get yourself there "whenever the church doors are opened," Mom pronounced, as though she was quoting one of the Ten Commandments.

"Now where does it say that in the Bible?" the old man demanded to know. Did a person have to be inside a building to worship? He'd nosed around in the Bible a good bit, and heard it quoted (and misquoted) all his life, and he knew that the early Christians never said anything about putting up buildings with electric lights and pulpits and songbooks and "all that there," as an old farmer down around Wakenda liked to say.

But when she was challenged by her agnostic husband, who had never even gotten around to "transferring his letter of membership" from Wakenda to the Kansas City congregation, she gave as good as she got. He needed chapter and verse, did he? Well, he'd get it. He'd met his match, and she was happy to oblige him. She could put her finger on the exact verse. (This battle had been fought many times over.) The Bible says, "in Hebrews," that we are not to be "forsaking the assembling of ourselves together."

"Now why couldn't that mean a simple meeting, say, in a cornfield, or out in the forest?" the doubter fired back.

"Well, it could. True Christians can meet almost anywhere." Scores of skirmishes had taught her to get "true" and "almost" in, or he'd jab back with something about meeting with the Methodists or the Salvation Army.

"What if they went in a tavern to preach, to read the Bible aloud, in hopes of saving some souls?" What did she think about that?

"Now you're mocking the Bible," she told him, her voice as flat and cold as glass. "You're getting pretty close to blasphemy!"

"I'm not mocking anything," he told her heatedly. "I'm discussing. Anyway, you've been known to get the Scriptures all balled up."

"Maybe I have, but I get the gist of it right every time, and you can't deny that," she told him, though he had denied it many times. And she knew that the Bible says, "Where two or three are gathered together in my name, there am I in the midst of them." That was enough for her. Church was where you would find a gathering of Church of Christ members. To Mom and the rest of the faithful even the name had to be right—or you were headed for eternal damnation.

"Now that business about the exact name is preposterous," said the old man.

Church. Always
church.

"The Bible doesn't say anything about Methodists or any of those other folks," Mom retorted. She was sorry for them, but they only had to read the Bible where it says, "The churches of Christ salute you."

She was bound and determined to get herself to church. "Even if I have to drive myself."

Of course a small boy had no say-so in the matter. On Sunday mornings I was roused from bed and told to get a move on. Mom hated being late; by getting there early she could get her favorite seat and catch up on gossip.

Services began at ten o'clock sharp and went full steam until noon, and sometimes a little later, depending on whether the preacher was long-winded. First came prayer and a hymn; then Bible study—little children off in separate rooms, teenagers downstairs, adults staying put. Later the saints reassembled to sing and pray, hear a sermon, and take communion—that is, "celebrate the Lord's Supper"—every Sunday, of course, for that too was spelled out in the Bible.

"We've heard much this morning to think about," Bro. Leonard Swearingin, or Bro. Churchill Teghtmeyer, or Bro. Roger Rinkenbaugh announced solemnly at the end. They were the church elders, men of serious faces and somber voices, blameless brethren. And their children too. If they slipped, an elder was stained and had to step down. "Train up a child in the way he should go: and when he is old, he will not depart from it." That's in Proverbs.

A godly man of ability and a desire to serve became a deacon. (Somewhere in the Bible there's talk of a "deaconess," but Mom's crowd had long ago decided to ignore that.) If a deacon remained pure and showed initiative, he might be elevated to an elder and put "in charge" of the church.

At the closing of each morning service one of the elders congratulated the preacher for having "brought us a sound message" and summarized the main points. This was done "for our mutual edification." An exceptional sermon brought higher praise. "We have heard God's word rightly divided." Yes, we've heard much that is "worthy of our consideration." (Partly to irritate Mom, the doubter dubbed Brother Swearingin, who also happened to be one of his bosses at the Ford Plant, "Old Bro. Worthy of Our Consideration.")

"Does anyone have news of the sick or the shut-ins?" How is Sister Gilbert doing? "She's on the mend, you say? Good." Is Brother Herbert laid up? (He's much younger than my grandmother, you see, and called by his first name.) "Yes," his wife replies, "they had to take out his gallbladder, but he's up and around now, though, and would appreciate cards and visitors." Thank you, Sister Thelma.

The womenfolk had news of the sick. This was their time to shine, to speak. This and during Bible study, though few women spoke up even then. Rules about who could speak and when weren't written down anywhere. They didn't need to be. Why not? Paul said to Timothy: "But I suffer not a woman to teach, nor to usurp authority over the man, but to keep silent." We speak where the Bible speaks. So it was in the smoothly working natural order of things that menfolk prayed, preached, led the singing, and "waited on the Lord's Table" with a short communion sermon.

Male or female, backslider or aspiring deacon, one's exact position and expected behavior in the church were known to one and all. Subtleties of language, surely a mystery to an outsider, abounded, conveying rules and codes, making it all seem perfectly natural. My old man, for instance, having never changed his membership, was never called "Brother Roy," and I was always "Sister Ruth's boy." Nor was Roy asked to lead the singing, or pray, or "wait on the table," or deliver a short message. That's good. He wouldn't have done any of those things. Nor did he "partake" of the body (the bread) and the blood (the grape juice) of Jesus or help take up the collection at communion.

The old man, zealously on the lookout for chinks in the full armor of Mom's righteousness, said he had doubts about the Church of Christ's use of many small cups of grape juice during communion. He recognized the health issue, he said mischievously. One cup per person was sanitary. But doesn't it say somewhere in the Bible that Jesus "took the cup, and gave thanks," before giving it to the faithful. "The Bible doesn't say anything about cups," the old man said, spoiling for a fight.

When Mom brushed this aside as so much silliness, he reminded her of the Kansas City congregation of defiant "one cuppers." They felt so strongly about following every word of the Bible that they engaged others in formal debate some years back. What did she think about that? Those one cuppers are "too extreme," Mom replied, and put the matter out of her mind.

But instrumental music was another matter. "Singing and making melody in your heart to the Lord"—the Bible says that. And that's what Mom and the Church of Christ declared boldly, sometimes belligerently, if anyone was deluded enough to suggest bringing in a piano or an organ. The Bible doesn't say anything about any piano, or a choir, for that matter. In the Church of Christ you sing. Yes, you. Everybody sings. Don't say you can't carry a tune: sing along with the rest—you'll get the tune going pronto. You'll sing. There is no choir, there is no soloist standing devoutly, proudly, in front making a great display of praising God by hitting high notes the rest of us can only dream about. You sing, you and everybody else in the church house. And you, young man, will learn to master the tuning fork and the pitch pipe and will lead the singing.

All those rules. All those duties, and all that Sunday church. Surely, that was enough. It was more than enough, for someone who had seen Big Red in the buff, and who loved swatting baseballs and jacking around with his buddies and had fallen for Friday night moviegoing and pinball playing, and who had inherited the old man's distaste for piety.

Sometimes we got even more church. Two or three times a year, Brother Teghtmeyer or another elder announced a "Protracted Meeting." Ouch! A Protracted Meeting meant one whole week, often two, of nightly services. That's right. Two weeks. Some evangelist, maybe one from far away, say from Iowa or Texas, would be arriving to preach every night, including Saturday if we could nab him for only a week.

Few, if any, expected to be revived in the way those "other" (and "wrong") churches did it—we didn't go in for whooping and hollering, or getting all emotional. We hoped our numbers would multiply and our influence grow. We were urged to persuade some of our neighbors or friends or fellow workers at Ford's or Sheffield Steel to join us. But we were a solemn people, and few outsiders came.

We were removed from the world. That was our glory, our victory over this world. There was a stately brick

Methodist church across the street; its members seemed a convivial lot as they mingled after services. But we ignored them, paying them as little mind as possible.

We exulted in our separation from all others, even those who called themselves Christian. On Christmas or Easter Sunday our evangelists began by saying they would not be preaching a "holiday" sermon. Why not? Every Lord's Day is special and commemorates the birth and death and resurrection of Our Savior. After those serious words we got a sermon much like every other Sunday: one that stressed our duties, our obligations, our faithfulness to the Word. And the great reward awaiting each of us in the next world.

Such were the messages of those two-week meetings. You talk about being protracted! Those revival meetings often came in the spring or the fall, and sometimes, at the same time, Vacation Bible School crucified summer days for a couple of weeks. Church, always church.

Few other kids on Thompson Street went to church of any kind. Why me? And why so much? Why, on a warm spring evening, just when I was in the middle of a good game of stickball, did my mother's shrill voice have to shatter the air with, "Boy, you come on in here. You come in here and get ready for church." Protracted Meetings even rode roughshod over Thompson Street's ritual of going Friday night to the picture show.

Sometime during the course of a Protracted Meeting— often as a way of kicking off the joyful week—the "brotherhood" treated itself to an "All Day Meeting." Oh, oh, oh. Gloom, despair, agony on me! No baseball, no pinball today. How those words burned the ears of one small boy. Those All Day Meetings were just that. Church all day.

But they included a marvelous feast. Every family, if they could, brought a "basket supper"—enough food to feed your own family. And some others. Keep in mind, brethren, that some of the old folks or the infirm are just making ends meet. Some are on strike or have been laid off. Some of the elderly have only their Social Security check to live on. So, remember: bring enough food to share with others.

Following the morning service during those All Day Meetings, the congregation moved across the street to a Masonic hall rented for such occasions. Why not just go downstairs and eat in the basement of the church, like folks at some other churches did? Not allowed. Some ancient elders at Twenty-sixth and Spruce—the congregation known to be "anti" just about everything—had decreed: "no fun or frivolity" in the church building, and that includes eating. Oh, I see. Do you have to have chapter and verse for everything? Guess so. But what about those many cups of grape juice? Never you mind about that.

The sisters went on ahead and prepared the feast. The menfolk milled about, smoking, swapping yarns about the gas mileage their new Ford or Chevy got. A few even drove Oldsmobiles or Buicks, but not many could afford those rich folks' cars. It was no accident that one of our favorite sermons spelled out in stern but head-nodding detail how it's "easier for a camel to go through the eye of a needle, than for a rich man to enter into the kingdom of God." That verse always brought vigorous nods from Mom and hearty Amens from the menfolk.

As Mom and the sisterhood prepared the food, little kids ran around playing tag—having fun and frivolity. Teenage boys, except those pondering whether they might want to be ordained evangelists themselves some-day, stood around in bunches hitting each other. "Hey, stop that horsing around! Remember where you are and what day of the week this is!"

The young girls went inside and helped set the tables while their mothers or grandmothers unloaded their bountiful basket suppers. In short order the long tables sagged under whole regiments of fried chicken, sweet potatoes, corn bread, green beans, macaroni salad, pick-led beets, meat loaf, baked ham, baked beans, and bat-talions of Jell-O salad. Mom turned out a premium pineapple upside-down cake. Think you could eat just one piece? Dare you to try!

Chow-down time. Hey, hold on there little man. You know you can't be grabbing food like that before Brother Max offers a word of thanks. Someday when you're grown up, you'll have to give the blessing. So, pay attention to what Cousin Max says.

All right boy, now you can start piling food on your plate. Children and old folks and those clinging to a walker or on crutches go first; then the menfolk—work-ingmen, men wearing their church-going suits, pass by filling their plates. The women stand by and watch. Satisfied. Dignified. Proud. They've earned this right to admire their labor and the hungry Christians. This was their version of "waiting on the table."

"My, my, Aunt Minnie, that's got to be your banana pudding! I could be a blind man and spot it. Make sure those big old boys there in front don't hog it all up."

"I've got a question for you, Sister Helen. Do you cook this good for Brother Ralph and your family every day? Ralph, your oldest boy's going to be bigger than you are before you know it."

Everyone, even the women when it came their turn, loaded their plates high in this glorious fellowship of food. It was cooking that went down deep into your soul. Those green beans, that banana pudding, told you that life was good in the ark of the church. And if you weren't too sure what God was, or whether there even was such a nay-saying, terrifying God as your kinfolks believed, well, then, that fried chicken and sweet custard pie pushed those troublesome thoughts away for a while.

Once the eating was done and the plates and cups had been cleaned up and the menfolk had stretched their legs and had a drag or two on a cigarette, it was time for more preaching and singing. And praying, too, of course. So, back across the street and into the church building. Those afternoon "lessons" were best kept short and to the point. Folks were too full to sit too long—"I'm stuffed to the gills, how about you?" Some of the elderly or overfed were nodding off.

Everybody on your feet. It's time for some singing. How about "Jesus Saves"? That'll get your juices flowing. Throw yourself into it and you'll work off a pound of two of that ham you lit into. For this rousing song of praise in three-quarter time, we need Bro. Ralph McGee. He's known far and wide in Church of Christ circles for his double chin, bald head, and fondness for quick tempos. "We have heard the joyful sound, Jesus saves! Jesus saves!"

More preaching. More singing. More praying. More Bible reading. After all that spiritual uplift, a body needs food. Time to march back across the street.

None for me. Come on, you can hold a small piece of cake or a slice of Sister Mary Margaret's pie. Your mother, as I recall, was also an extra good hand at mincemeat.

You talk about good! Oh, go on boy, have some more fried chicken, have that drumstick there. It's got your name written all over it. You're a growing boy. Thanks, don't mind if I do, Uncle Fred.

Surely this All Day Meeting, this marathon, is over. Right? Nope. Brethren, flick those cigarettes away; sisters, clear away the plates and tuck the leftovers in the baskets. Everyone, head back across the street for the evening service. That's right, more.

After another sermon, more singing and praying, and one last call for backsliders to come forward and "make their wrongs right," finally, it was all over.

"What a glorious day," Mom pronounced as we rode home. Grandma Gilbert, tuckered out by the length of the day but not about to say so, agreed and would have said, "Amen." But women, even those in their seventh or eighth decades as stalwarts of the one true church, seldom said Amen, even outside the church building.

Dad usually just smoked as he drove along. What was there to say? And what was the use? He was thinking about hitting the hay; he had to face the assembly line early the next morning. In spring and summer I sprawled in the backseat and thought about all the baseballs I could have smacked that afternoon or the games I might have racked up down at Frank's.

As I rode along in silence I was often thinking uncomfortable thoughts about Mom's world. Surely, all other people—those Methodists across the street, those Catholics in Little Italy—wouldn't burn in hell forever just because they got their church name wrong, would they? How could that be? And what about people off in distant lands, places like Russia or Korea? What kind of God was it who decreed that Mr. Jim and Mrs. Strange and even kids on Thompson Street were bound for the fiery furnace? Hey, Mr. Jim was just as good a person as anyone in Mom's church, maybe better. Yeah, better.

I'll show them someday. I'll quit going to church as soon as I'm big enough—and have the courage to stand up to Mom. Oh, maybe I won't quit all of sudden, and cause a big commotion. To tell the truth, I'll probably take the old man's route and drift away, hoping no one says too much.

Still, it was one thing to plan some sort of tippy-toed jailbreak while trying to make out a case, however silently, for my friends and heroes, like Mr. Jim. It was another thing, a very big thing, to know how firmly Mom's church had clamped its hand on my shoulder and told me what "true" religion was. Even today, the hymns come back to me whenever they will. They float in space and nosedive into my heart anytime they want. Is that my mother singing? I begin to hum or sing or whistle the chorus. I can't help it. For a second I am back there in the church.

Little or none of that did I understand as we rode home after a full day of services. But even so I couldn't help wondering about the sanity of whoever dreamed up the idea of the All Day Meeting and the Protracted Meeting scheduled to start tomorrow night, Monday, and run triumphantly night after night. Oh, Lord. Could a body endure it?

10

"Bees That Have No Sting"

W hen Bro. Hobart Stretch stepped into the pulpit to speak that summer night many years ago he was doing his duty as a man and as a loyal member of the Church of Christ. He was not a preacher. Brother Stretch was a barber by trade, reputedly a good one, though he was far too modest to talk up his mastery of scissors, razor, talcum, and Vitalis. No, Brother Hobart was a plain man, a salt-of-the-earth type, said my mother, who confused his names and called him "Homer Strich."

"The man's name is Hobart," Dad roared every time she mangled his name. "And it's Stretch, not Strich. Hobart Stretch!"

"That's what I said," Mom replied, "Homer Strich."

That drove the old man crazy. He searched around for a pencil and some paper and wrote, even printed in capital letters, H O B A R T and demanded that she pronounce it correctly. Then he printed S T R E T C H. "There now, can you say the man's name correctly? There's no such name as 'Strich.'" He found it embarrassing, he said, to hear her say it wrong. Could she get it right?

Well, yes and no. For a while she called him Hobart Strich. Sometimes it was Homer Stretch. But let some time go by, and she slipped back into her old ways, even greeting the poor man as Homer and introducing him as Bro. Homer Strich.

Did Bro. Hobart Stretch find it as irritating as the old man did, or did he even notice? Probably not. The same qualities that allowed Brother Stretch to accept my mother's lapses prompted him to agree to deliver a short message to the brotherhood. So when an elder peered out over the congregation to say that Brother Stretch or some similar stalwart had agreed to speak, the announcement was that one of our brothers in Christ would be "occupying the time."

We needed the Hobart Stretches of this world. The Spruce congregation didn't hold with the "One Man Pastor System," sometimes called the "located minister." Never mind that the vast majority of Churches of Christ in the city and in the nation comfortably assumed that employing a minister wouldn't send them straight to hell. But to us, those churches were dead wrong, and they would find out just how far from the straight and narrow they were come Judgment Day.

Many devout words, some of them heated and all of them utterly sincere, had been spoken and written in the great fight over the One Man Pastor System. Mom and the two or three hundred souls at the Spruce church felt so strongly against this located minister business that they had to have long discussions with themselves about whether they could "fellowship" anyone from one of those other churches.

Tough decision. Some of those who had fallen for the

heresy of the One Man Pastor System were kinfolk or acquaintances from way back. They were good folks, and we loved them—much as we loved other moral people out there in the world—and we would do anything in our power for them, but could we offer them the right hand of fellowship? Could we worship with them or allow one of their located ministers to come and preach to us? The answer had to be no. We speak where the Bible speaks.

Just where the Bible did speak on this thorny issue was absolutely clear—depending upon which side had your ear, of course. The factions in the Kansas City Churches of Christ agreed to tackle the question in a formal debate. Might as well thrash out this business once and for all.

Oh, it was a great debate. I know. I was there at the massive Ivanhoe Temple on Linwood Boulevard. This was a ritzy part of town where some of the houses looked like mansions and the folks who lived in them could afford to shop at the nearby snazzy Country Club Plaza. Mom made me go. Every night. The huge auditorium was packed almost to capacity.

We brought in a straight-shootin' young Texan, Bro. Leroy Garrett, a high school teacher by profession who roamed far and wide to preach. Our stern Texan was opposed by a south Missourian, William J. Humble, just twenty-eight years old, who'd mastered the same King James Bible and didn't flinch from doing his debating duty.

For four nights they talked. Solemnly. First one man and then the other hammered home his points with Scripture and logic. Pastor Humble introduced the words of academic bigwigs from the divinity schools of Yale,

Harvard, and the University of Chicago. Our Brother Garrett acknowledged these were mighty men, but they were in error, for all their lofty degrees. ("You know what that Ph. and D. stands for, don't you?" one of my favorite cousins whispered to me—"Piled Higher and Deeper.") The debaters were dignified and civil. Each was eloquent, but Mom saw clearly that Brother Garrett was a lot more polished. More persuasive.

As the crowd spilled out into the streets each evening, God-fearing folks huddled in groups and went over the major points. Surely, their man had carried the day, converted the audience, or at least anyone who was "open-minded" and "willing to follow the Bible." That's what Mom and all my cousins thought about Brother Garrett. She expected to see, why, "no telling how many" coming over from the other side to join the Spruce bunch and their allies in the great fight for souls.

"Don't count on it," the old man said sardonically.

"And why is that?" Mom demanded to know. She had never heard the case against the One Man Pastor System or church-supported colleges made so forcefully in all her born days.

"Because all those other folks are just like you! They came with their minds made up," Dad told her sharply. "They are no more going to change their minds, no matter what this Leroy Garrett says, than you are."

"Oh, I don't know about that!" Mom fired back. She was one of Brother Garrett's great admirers, and she had a hunch that the power of his words would turn even the hardest heart.

"It's not about anyone having a hard heart," the old man told her. "People have already made up their minds on this issue and every issue. Be honest! Haven't you made up your mind? Are you going to sit here and tell me that this Humble fellow could have done or said anything that would have caused you to think again?"

Mom, earnest, optimistic, and straight in the faith, hated this kind of discussion. She had no doubt she had an open mind. She also knew what the truth was. People with a truly open mind would see it her way. She wasn't about to be budged. Dad had lost the war years ago, but he could no more restrain himself from firing a few shots at Mom's fortress of belief than she could have said, yes, I see, I've been wrong for fifty years on the One Man Pastor System, and so were my folks, and all of my kinfolks in the one true church.

Without a "located minister," the Spruce church had to call on faithful men from the congregation to speak when the ordained evangelists were busy elsewhere. Bro. Hobart Stretch could be counted on to "occupy the time." If his business didn't give him time during the day to sit in his barber chair and rummage through the Bible for some verses and a sermon topic, he made time after work. Mom often pointed to Brother Homer—"the man's name is Hobart!"—as an example of how every Christian had something to give.

So it was that Bro. Homer Strich—as some small part of me prefers to remember him—stepped gamely into the pulpit that evening more than forty years ago. His message, he said, as he turned to write out the title of his remarks on the blackboard, was "Bees That Have No Sting." He opened his Bible and glanced at the sympathetic souls he had known for years—many of whom had sat in his barber chair and profited from his tonsorial dexterity.

He wanted to say, he announced solemnly, a few

words about "Bees That Have No Sting." But there was some problem. He thumbed through his Bible, saying nothing, looking up from time to time as though to nod to the congregation that he would be with us in a moment. He continued rifling through his Bible. He appeared to be frantically looking for something. The congregation waited, in silence. What was he looking for, his notes, his sermon outline?

He didn't say. After what seemed an eternity, Brother Stretch closed his Bible, looked squarely at the congregation, and stammered his way through a homily on some topic now long forgotten. But what is still clear is that his remarks had nothing to do with bees or stings or anything even remotely connected to his title scrawled across the blackboard.

At the end, one of the elders finished the service and thanked Bro. Hobart Stretch for having "occupied the time." Driving home, Dad needled Mom without mercy. "That was a wonderful sermon we had heard tonight from Hobart, though did I miss something?" The old man was puzzled; he could swear there was something missing. "Oh, I remember now." Hobart had not said one thing about "bees that have no sting."

"All right, all right," Mom fired back. "It's mighty easy to mock. Not everybody's a great preacher."

Mom knew the sower of doubt was up to his old tricks. Mere titles didn't mean much. It was the message that counted. And she'd heard some sound gospel preached by Bro. Homer Strich.

11

Buck's Boy

I t was much easier for my father and me to chuckle at poor Bro. Hobart Stretch's pulpit lapses than for us to figure out a way to laugh together, or even to smile at life in concert. Whether Dad ever really wanted to connect any of those dots—many of which could hardly be seen with the naked eye—that remained between us, I can't say. We were so different. He always seemed old to me; he was in his fifties when I was in my teens. It seemed perfectly natural to refer to him as "my old man." Every boy I knew called his father that—not in a spirit of meanness, or affection. Just as a description, that's all. I knew no one who actually liked his father or spent any time with him.

He was the North Pole; I was the South. I was loud; he was quiet. He was short; I was tall. And tall early on. I sprouted to six feet and an inch more by the time I was thirteen, in 1952, the year he turned fifty. He was balding; I had hair. He was pudgy and stocky; so was I until my growing spurt meant I could tower over him. I liked to loll in bed in the morning; he always got up early.

He loved to get out his toolbox and have a go at a defective water pump or carburetor on one of our various cars. I preferred to play catch or talk to Mr. Jim. With tools in hand, the old man made major improvements to every room of our little house, even adding stylish extensions to the kitchen and back bedroom. When I borrowed his tools, even his prized ones, I somehow managed to leave them out in the backyard or lose them.

I liked to tease, to make up nicknames; he thought little in life was funny. He was usually serious, laughing now and then, but not often, and only around grown-ups. He regarded baseball as stupid beyond belief, and me as equally stupid. He wasn't completely wrong.

He viewed life bleakly, through a glass darkly. When he did talk to me he couldn't get finished with going on about the Depression. He would have bet good money that my generation of doughnut eaters wouldn't last a second should hard times come again. His mind was ensnared in the harshness of the past; mine was entranced by the rays of those radiant days when I would don a Yankee uniform.

I was callow and insensitive to his life; his harangues about the thirties left me wondering how much longer I had to sit and listen to him. That he was Buck's boy, I knew; that his mother was emotionally cold, I knew that, too. But it didn't register with my self-absorbed adolescent mind how grim and dark his past was, how being Buck's boy was too heavy for anyone to lug around. That he was like Buck in so many ways didn't soften my teenager's cold, hard heart.

I also knew that he and Mom were hopelessly mismatched and that divorce was unthinkable. But I could no more have understood my father than I could have predicted the Second Coming. All I knew, or cared to know, was that he was a man in whom the elements of life were chaotically mixed, jumbled beyond my comprehension.

He had talents. But I either ignored them or foolishly took them for granted. He knew sign language and "talked" regularly with the Tompkinses, a family who lived next door to Mr. Jim. They were "deaf and dumb," sealed off from everyone else by an awful wall of silence and forced to scribble notes frantically to outsiders whenever they needed something. Once I asked Dad how he had learned to "speak on his fingers," as he put it. He said tersely that he'd had a friend once who was deaf. "He taught me." The old man didn't want to talk about it.

Years later I learned that his friend had been a farm boy his age with a terrible fondness for liquor. When he drank he grunted angrily, desperately trying to talk. One night, drunk, he stumbled on the railroad tracks that cut through Wakenda, fell down, and passed out. Then tragedy. An incoming freight train ran over him, mangling his body, killing him instantly.

I knew only that whenever our neighbors had a problem they came to my dad. With fingers flying they stood on the front porch or in the backyard, expressing sounds none of the rest of us could hear.

No, he never asked me whether I wanted to learn how to sign. Or suggested that I learn. Never. But did I ever show the slightest interest in learning even a few basic signs? Never.

But in some ways he tried to reach out to me. Every so often in my pudgy years before I took my growing spurt, he would abruptly announce on a Saturday or

Sunday morning that later in the day we were going to hear the Kansas City Philharmonic in concert.

What? Can this be true? I mean, no one's father, not on Thompson Street, not in blue-collar Northeast, ever went to hear the symphony orchestra. No one I knew, anyway. The first couple of times he made his astounding announcement I replied lamely that I'd heard the Philharmonic play, that our school made us go. We were bused to Municipal Auditorium once or twice a year to hear the orchestra. (I didn't tell him that we always misbehaved and mocked "the maestro," Hans Schwieger, and his long flopping hair.)

But Dad was not to be put off. He'd made up his mind that he wanted to hear some music and that I was going with him. That was it. (He wasn't given to explaining himself, certainly not to me: once I ran in and said I had heard about this great baseball camp down in the Ozarks run by a old ballplayer named Zach Wheat—"he's in the Hall of Fame"—and could I possibly go for a week? "No!" my father replied and walked away.) So, did I have to go and listen to an orchestra play all that longhair music? "Yes!"

He insisted that I scrub my face, comb my hair, and put on a dress shirt and a pair of my church-going slacks— "they don't allow blue jeans down there, you know." And anyway, we didn't want to look like a couple of farmers, did we? I didn't tell him as he put on his clip-on tie and we headed out the door that we always looked like a couple of hicks from the sticks.

We always sat high up in the balcony, in the cheap seats of that stately, cavernous downtown music hall. Dad claimed he could hear more of the orchestra up there. He demanded that I keep quiet. No yawning. No squirming. And I was not to applaud each time the orchestra stopped playing. "Lots of these pieces have three or four movements, and you are not supposed to clap until the whole symphony has been played." I had no intention of applauding.

Of course, I never saw a familiar face. When I told kids on the block or at school what torments I had endured they looked at me blankly. Your old man must be off his rocker!

We usually rode home in silence, staring out the window. I didn't know any boys who actually talked to their dads. Chattering away about the music would have been, well, weird. Oh, occasionally he tried to explain what we had heard. But not often. Thank God. I certainly wasn't going to say anything about that music or that guy Schwieger. Who was he, a German? I thought we were supposed to hate Germans.

In time, when I became older, bigger, and a bona fide galoot, he stopped making me go with him. He knew by then that on any given weekend day I was likely to have a baseball game or something I said I had to do. We stood on different shores, distant strangers to each other—not every second, but most of the time. I remained convinced that he didn't understand me, and didn't care, and probably didn't even like me.

But he was an enigma. Every now and then he got out an old harmonica, one he'd had since he was a boy. After inspecting it he would play a few notes—and put it back in the case. But when he took a mind to play, to stay with a tune and even fool around with some variations on the melody, he went to the basement. There he played up a storm, sometimes for hours. He could play ragtime tunes and Dixieland songs. Now and then I sat on the top of the basement stairs and listened and wondered.

But don't ask him to play at a gathering, say, of the cousins sitting on the front porch. That would be dumb. All requests got a sharp "No!" If pressed by my mother, he retaliated that he had no talent and that he wasn't going to offend anyone's ears with his "caterwauling"— where he got that word I'll never know. Caterwauling or not, that was the end of the matter.

He could also, after a fashion, play the fiddle. He had a beautiful miniature violin that he kept tucked away on the top shelf of the front bedroom closet. He got it down when the spirit moved him, which wasn't often, and took himself down to the basement, where he played Irish jigs and reels and bits of bluegrass numbers.

Did we ever talk about his music or whether he might teach me to play the harmonica or the fiddle? No. We remained faithful to our self-imposed code of silence. My mind was a million miles away, dreaming about Yankee Stadium, or that new pinball machine down at Frank's Filthy Restaurant, or something else equally foreign to the world of my father.

He baffled me. He could really play the harmonica— but vehemently denied that he had any talent whatso- ever. His fiddle playing wasn't bad. He was also a pretty fair artist, able to sketch likenesses quickly. But he crum- pled up his every drawing and pitched it in the waste- basket, "where it belonged."

He was a card-carrying Democrat who voted for "Ike and prosperity" in 1956. He was a self-proclaimed agnostic and hated going to church, but said sharply he wouldn't ever vote for any Catholic—and didn't when John F. Kennedy ran in 1960. You mean he actually voted for Nixon the Republican? Yeah. According to the doubting Thomas, Catholics couldn't be trusted. They take their orders from the Pope.

He admired FDR and swore by the New Deal—"that and the war got us out of the Depression!" But he loathed Socialism ("just watered down Communism," remember.) To those who thought they hankered to live under Socialism (though no mortal on Thompson Street or anywhere in Northeast was ever heard to express any such cockamamy sentiment), he had a ready reply. "Just go downtown and try to reason with the gas company or Kansas City Power and Light." This pronouncement came from the same man who often announced that most of America's social problems could be greatly alleviated if every young couple, on the day of their marriage, was given a house by the government. No, he admitted, a free house wouldn't solve everything, but it would sure help more than most ideas people came up with.

Another of his strongly felt maxims was that all people should be judged and rewarded solely on their own merits. But he also was given to blurting out that "niggers" got exactly what they deserved—especially those down South, those "troublemakers," that "crowd Martin Luther King and other rabble-rousers were stirring up." Didn't they know that whites didn't want to associate with them?

Who was he? Well, he was sort of a wild Missouri jackass, one of those farm boys who wasn't a big talker but had opinions on everything. He was one of those untamed midwesterners who thought it was his inalienable right to speak his mind. It's a free country, isn't it? No one on Thompson Street or down at Ford's would disagree with him about that.

But he was Buck's boy. And like Buck, who had never amounted to anything, neither had Roy Roosevelt. Who said so? The old man said so. And many, many times. "I'm a failure. I've never accomplished anything of note and never will. My life hasn't amounted to a hill of beans." How many times did I hear him say that? Hundreds, thousands; sometimes it seemed liked millions.

"Now it's true, you haven't amounted to much," Mom replied as though on cue—this argument got reenacted often. "And neither have I. But, like you, I never had any education, any to speak of, that is. And no opportunities. My folks took me out of school at the end of the eighth grade. I'm not blaming them, not one little bit. Mom and Dad didn't see any reason for more education for a girl. And I was needed at home, to do farm chores."

"So you would have become something really big, is that it, if you had some more education? Is that your point?" he demanded to know.

"I don't know what I might have become. Maybe I would have become somebody important. I'm not saying I would have. I'm just saying that I never got a chance."

"Oh come on, what have you ever done that would suggest that you have any great intelligence or ability to rise above the common clod?"

"Listen, I'm not saying that I definitely would have risen very high. I'm just saying the truth, and you know it's the truth, that I never had a chance to find out what I could do. And neither did you."

Now the old man's dander was up. He wasn't about to let her get away with saying that if only she'd had a chance she would have soared. But he also wasn't open to any excuses for his own failure. He blamed himself, and himself alone: "I failed because I didn't have any gumption. I had no aim in life."

"But Roy, you never had any opportunities," Mom insisted. Maybe this time she could get him convinced.

He would have none of it. And all in all he thought it was a good thing he had lacked any drive to succeed. "To accomplish anything you have to have some brains—and I don't. I'm ordinary. I've never had any talent. That's the end of it."

If only it had been the end of it. It wouldn't have been so bad if he hadn't insisted on extending his harsh realism to those closest to him. But he was one of those, he explained, "who would tell you the truth, even if the truth hurt, and you didn't want to hear it."

Watch out. Don't transgress, don't screw up in any way. If you do, you're going to hear about it from the old man. Getting a little tubby? He'd be first in line to tell you that you were getting "fat." What's that? You're mumbling something about cutting back, or going on a diet? He'd wish you luck, but he'd have to be honest and tell you that he'd observed your fondness for gravy and cake.

The fact that he was pudgy most of his life only encouraged him to be ruthlessly "honest" with you. Being someone who had never amounted to anything, who couldn't even keep his own waistline under control, somehow justified his attacks on your weaknesses. He, too, had a fondness for cake and fried potatoes—but he admitted it! His willingness, even eagerness, to indict and convict himself worked in some unknown way to shield him—no need for you to criticize him: he had beaten you to the punch.

Money trickled through his fingers like water. "I'm no good managing money," he would say in a confession

Dad would
tell you the
truth, even if
the truth hurt.

that bordered on bragging. But if you gave signs of being careless with a dollar, boy, could you expect to get an earful from him. His failures and his eagerness to acknowledge them gave him license to ferret out weaknesses in others, even in their moments of triumph, however minor. Hit a home run, earn an admiring comment from someone, or be chosen to be the student conductor for one selection of the Northeast High School Band's spring concert, and you could expect to hear about how much you liked the spotlight.

"Watch out, boy! Looks to me like you want to be a big shot. You'll get the big head if you don't watch out."

Oh my God! Actually conduct the band for one measly Sousa march. Or hit a home run as a fourteen year old! You might come to like the spotlight a lot. You might yearn to become a Big Shot! You don't want that. You'll get the Big Head. And nothing could be worse than that. Stay a Little Shot. Admit your failure, tell others about it. Then you won't get the Big Head.

So, don't let the old man suspect that you dream of being somebody someday—I made the mistake early on of letting him in on my dream of playing baseball. "Listen, buster," he reminded me countless times, "you're not going to make the big leagues. You're going to have to work for a living just like me. Get that through your head."

Sometime during my junior year in high school he began to surprise me by asking, "How are you doing in school?" Uh, oh. That question was a stick of dynamite, usually tossed at me during dinner. Never once was his question a warm-up for wanting to know how was I doing in band or on the basketball team.

In two years, he and Mom came to one game. What a game to pick! That night I missed eight consecutive free throws and, late in the game, clumsily dribbled the ball on the out-of-bounds line. During time out, Coach Huhn flailed me with a towel. The next night, Mom was still "madder than a wet hen" at that "awful man." The old man said that he didn't see any bruises on me, that my appetite seemed good, and that "Northeast probably lost that game because of you, boy."

But who cared about that. Wasn't it grade card time? His tone was menacing now. The first time or two he asked to see my grade card I pointed cheerfully to my high marks in band and orchestra and wood shop. Those weren't important! He demanded to know how I was doing in history and English and math. I mumbled that I was doing okay, that I had passing marks of M and was on target to graduate. "Graduate! Doesn't every idiot and moron at Northeast graduate?" He had me there.

"M is for Medium," he shouted. Didn't I know where the Mediums of this world end up? They go right to the assembly line or the steel mill. "You've seen the line, boy, do you want to end up like me?" He then lambasted me for what seemed an eternity. If only there'd been an ounce of tenderness beneath his terrible honesty. He was obviously trying to bludgeon me into seeing the error of my ways before it was too late. But he never said a single word about school the next day, the next week, or any time before the next grade card came out.

Once in a great while, he and Mom came to a baseball game. She sat in the car, saying she didn't like to be in the sun—and didn't understand baseball. He strolled around having a smoke. Neither of them cared whether my team won or lost or how I did. No. Mom hoped we won because losing put me in a foul mood. "You've got to learn to be a good loser," she told me. "It's only a game."

One hot Saturday afternoon we were playing a team from the south part of Kansas City. We knew many of their players from high school games—and we hated them because they were rich, arrogant, and had fanatical fathers who cheered them on. Deep down, we feared they were better than we were, better in every way—and that's why they usually beat us. But today we were on the verge of victory.

Their fathers, who sat behind home plate and routinely abused our players, were angry their boys were losing. They took out their rage on me as I took our pitcher's warm-up tosses and readied myself for the last inning. A catcher now, I squatted there listening to abuse from men who were probably doctors and lawyers; I glanced down the right-field line. There off in the distance was my old man wearing his one suit, his clip-on tie, and his hat and standing under a shade tree. He and Mom had been to a funeral and had stopped by the game on the way home. Wisps of cigarette smoke floated above his head. He was reading a newspaper, just waiting for the game to be over. It went on a little longer than either of us hoped. The rich boys scored three runs and beat us. On the way home he said, "That wild throw of yours in the last inning didn't help any."

And yet, some of his behavior bordered on the comical. For all of his assertions about his inability to believe in God—sometimes said harshly, sometimes with a note of anguish—he complained every December when Kansas City started to decorate for the holiday season that the "true spirit" of Christmas was being lost. He railed against Consumerism. Commercialization was killing the spirit.

"Don't get me anything for Christmas," he barked each year. "Save your money." He meant it, too. Then, on Christmas Eve, just hours before the stores closed, he dashed downtown and bought gifts for everyone, often ignoring the price. For all his protestations, he greatly enjoyed giving presents. There wasn't a greedy, selfish bone in his body.

He observed his own rituals. When I finished the eighth grade in 1953, he, quite out of the blue, made a big deal out of the fact and marched me to downtown Kansas City and bought an expensive Bulova wristwatch for me. He gladly plopped down $45.00. That was almost half a week's salary then.

Did I want a watch? Had I ever said I did? No. Never. My opinion didn't matter. He wanted me to have a good watch. But nobody I knew wore a wristwatch. "Neat Guys" (our 1950s expression for nerds) wore watches, and so did our teachers, but nobody who was cool would be caught dead wearing one. I put my Bulova in the drawer and never took it out.

But geez-o-man, was he murder to buy for. Give him something, and you knew that his old ruthless honesty would come out sooner or later. Buy him a fancy silk tie, or a fashionable scarf, and give it to him for his birthday or Christmas. He would unwrap it, remove it, study it for a moment, then look you straight in the eye and say, "Well, I can see you might wear this sort of thing, but I won't."

"Now Roy, that's not a nice thing to say." That's Mom speaking her part. "You're making a snap judgment. I think it's very becoming."

No, he didn't think so. And no, he wouldn't be changing his mind. He didn't wear that kind of tie or scarf. He would hand it back to you and say, "I'm just being honest. I don't like it. You take it."

Years later when he lay in a hospital bed dying from emphysema and lung cancer I made a hurried automobile trip back from my home a thousand miles away. When I arrived at his room we exchanged pleasantries between his bouts of coughing and labored breathing. He told me—not coldly but not warmly either—that I shouldn't have bothered to come. Don't you have classes to teach?

Mom took me aside and said that he needed some new pajamas, since he was likely to be in the hospital for a while, and would I go get them. She looked in her purse for the money. She couldn't see the agony destroying the composure I had managed to keep on my face. Even on his deathbed he would hate whatever pajamas I picked out. He did, too.

And yet, and yet. . . . His makeup included a certain redeeming madness, the unpredictability of a true individualist, the wildness of a Missouri jackass.

He loved cars, brand-new, shiny automobiles. Better still, he loved buying new cars. And his favorite time to trade and buy a new one was late in the summer, soon after the new models hit the showrooms. When the car dealers announced their "late summer blockbuster sales," saying they'd stay open late, even all night, if need be, to clear their showrooms—that's when he got the yen to trade. "Trade up," he said. You could tell when he was beginning to get the itch. For several days he would say, after getting home from work, "Let's run over by that dealer who's announced a big sale."

He would begin by circling the lot slowly. Then he parked the car and strolled around the used cars before making a beeline for the new ones in the showroom. "Just lookin'," he waved to the eager salesmen. "Just lookin'."

He wasn't just looking. He was thinking. Figuring in his mind. He liked looking at all models and makes, but mainly Chevrolets and Fords. But since he worked at Ford's, he told himself, he ought to buy a Ford. That was the intelligent thing to do. But he was still thinking. Those new Pontiacs were honeys.

Then, without warning, he sprang like a tiger. As we were driving home from church on Sunday evening he said, "Let's take another look at those new models."

He "traded up" on several Sunday evenings: the 1954 and 1955 Fords.

Mom's objection that it was the Lord's Day and that she had to get up and go to work in the morning, "and so do you, Roy," didn't cut any ice with him. He said there was nothing in the Bible that said a fellow had to refrain from looking at some automobiles on Sunday. Or even buying one if the ghost of Henry Ford moved him.

The spirit guided his mind on several Sunday evenings. He "traded up" to a new 1952 Ford; two years later he got himself a nice 1954, a Ford of course. One year later, he had to have a red-and-white 1955; two years later he convinced himself he needed that new Ford Fairlane, the one with the tail fins and twin exhaust system.

The spirit could move him in wondrous ways when it came to automobiles. I turned sixteen on a Monday in March 1955. On the following Sunday evening as we rode home from church the old man announced that we would swing by a used car lot that he knew was open; he'd had his eye on a car there, a black 1949 Chevrolet.

"But, Roy, what do we need with a second car?" Mom demanded to know.

Never mind about that, he told her, this '49 Chevy was a doozy.

We pulled into the used car lot, parked, and made straight for the Chevy. It was in immaculate condition inside and out. The old man lifted the hood and checked out the fan belts; he opened the driver's door and sat behind the wheel beaming. He asked the lurking salesman for the keys and said we wanted to take it for a spin.

Dad drove it a mile or two, taking it up several hills to give it the real test, and then said I should take the wheel for a few minutes.

"Do you like it?" the old man asked me as we pulled

back into the lot. "Sure, it's great," I answered, wondering why he had any interest in it.

The used car salesman said he thought it was a steal at $250.00. If he expected to haggle, he was happily disappointed. The old man agreed that the price was right, pulled out his checkbook, and wrote a check for the full amount. I ambled back to the car where Mom sat, biting her tongue. He wasn't a man to tangle with when he bought an automobile, even a second one we sure didn't need.

"You might as well drive it home, boy," Dad said. "It's your car." That was it. No hugs or outpourings of congratulations on becoming sixteen, but no admonitions about safe driving, either. He handed me the keys and we shook hands on the transaction. Man to man. I drove my sleek Chevy home, thinking not so much about the old man as about the twin pipes and low rum-

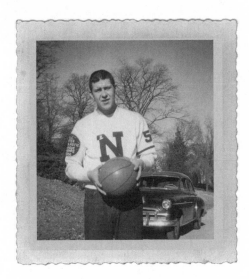

"You might as well drive it home, boy. It's your car."

bling mufflers I intended to install immediately. In the twinkling of an eye, and without any promises having been extracted from me about being careful or without anything having been said about my miserable grades, the old man bought a car for his worthless son.

Why? Well, he said if I had my own car I wouldn't be bothering him to drive his still-new 1955 Ford. True enough. But the real reason probably went deeper, much deeper, down into the soul of a Missouri boy who had treated himself to a brand-new Model T almost the day he got out of the navy. I think he believed, almost religiously, that every young man should have a car, a nice one if possible. Just as soon as the law allowed. It was Sunday after all.

12

The Bowery Boys
Original Dixieland Jazz Band

M y father and I agreed on one thing: Dixieland jazz. I have no idea when or where the old man first came to love that two-beat music out of New Orleans, but love it he did. And so did I. He played it often on his "table console," and always loud. Loud was the best way to listen to all good music, he said. That way you don't miss a thing; you hear every note.

I agreed. Crank it up. Let her rip.

But did he always have to pick Saturday or Sunday morning to let her rip? He did. Weekend mornings, beginning about eight o'clock, was his favorite time to rock the house with some version of "Fidgety Feet" or "Muskrat Ramble" or "Chinatown."

"Turn that thing down," Mom yelled. "What are you trying to do, wake up the whole neighborhood?"

For once I agreed with her. As a no-account teenager I jammed my head under the pillow, resolving each time to do the impossible—to shut out the music and sleep some more. But not even a loathsome adolescent could sleep through that mound of sound. I knew I might as

Dad standing by the backyard incinerator: he preferred to smash and burn the offending record.

well get up when my feet began to fidget and I felt myself waiting for the trombone solos, most of which I could hum note for note. Yeah, for God's sake, what was he trying to do, wake up the whole neighborhood?

"If they are not up yet, they ought to be," Dad snapped back. He'd been up for several hours, had already damn near coughed his lungs out, had his breakfast, smoked a half dozen cigarettes, and read the newspaper. Time to get on with the day.

It wasn't always Dixieland. Symphonic music, particularly if it featured the brass section, was fine with him, but good 78 rpm recordings of orchestras or brass groups were hard to find, particularly where he shopped. He preferred to rummage around in the record bins down at Katz Drugstore or in the music section at Sears or Monkey Wards. When he found a good version of marches, preferably majestic John Philip Sousa pieces, he put those on the record player and peeled the paint off the walls. Do you have any idea what it feels like to be blasted out of bed early in the morning by "Semper Fidelis" or "The Stars and Stripes Forever?"

One hot summer morning when I stumbled from my room, with eyes full of sleep and hair askew, the old man looked up and said he'd played that last number just for me. "Do you know what it is? I'll give you a hint: it's by Sousa. You've probably played it in the marching band." Before I could mumble a guess, he announced with a wicked grin that it was "High School Cadets." What did I think about that? I didn't think he would want to hear my murderous thoughts.

When he bought a record he played it the moment he walked into the house. If it suited his taste, he played it over and over, and loud. If it offended him in any way, he snatched it from the turntable, marched to the backyard, and broke it over his knee. Then he threw it into the brick trash incinerator, doused it with lighter fluid, and set it afire.

"That's a fine way to waste good money," Mom scolded.

"It's no good. I don't want it in the house," he told her sternly.

"But hold your wild horses," Mom demanded. Shouldn't he listen to it a few more times? "Maybe it will grow on you. Maybe you'll come to like it, just a little bit. I tell you money is too hard to come by to waste like that."

"No," he thundered. "I've heard enough to know that I don't like it—and never will. That's it. I won't have it in the house. Keeping it around won't bring back the money."

His mind was made up. What he liked, he loved; what he didn't, he hated. Better to smash and burn the offending record and be done with it once and for all.

I inched closer to getting on his good side by bringing home a Turk Murphy recording I'd found at Jenkins Music Company. At Jenkins, the big downtown store where you could buy anything from sheet music to a Steinway piano, customers were allowed to take records into booths and preview them. (Jenkins was a teenagers' paradise on rainy or cold Saturday afternoons.) I listened to both sides of the new LP—long playing—vinyl record to make sure that Turk Murphy and his San Francisco Jazz Band wouldn't give offense. The old man might not love Murphy's rough, tailgate trombone style, but even he couldn't hate Murphy's foot-stomping "Red Flannel Rag" and "Cake Walkin' Babies from Home."

"Where'd you get that?" he wanted to know when I put the new record on.

Get a camera! Hold the fort! He was actually smiling.

"Jenkins," I said. "You should check it out sometime if you're ever downtown."

He said he didn't get down there very often but if they had any more of those Murphy records to pick up another. He reached in his pocket and handed me some money. "Well, now, there, then," I muttered in my best James Dean imitation. Was the old man actually saying he trusted my judgment, that I wasn't, at least this once in my life, a total nincompoop?

I brought home other foot-stomping Turk Murphy

recordings. I found some hot "Muggsy" Spanier and Bob Scobey LPs. Each passed the test. The old man liked them a lot. He played them, and played them loud.

I scored a coup when I brought home an album called "Coast Concert" with Bobby Hackett on cornet, the one and only Jack Teagarden on trombone, and Matty Matlock on clarinet. The moment I put it on to play the old man was entranced. He listened intently to both sides—from "Muskrat Ramble" to "Basin Street Blues." When side two finished he said, "Let's hear it again. But turn it up some."

Mom said dinner was on the table. We'd better come before the fried chicken got cold. Dad waved her away, saying he wanted to hear this brand-new record one more time. He sat there transfixed, listening carefully to every note. At the end he looked up and said that that was the greatest Dixieland sound he'd ever heard in his life. "What did you pay for it? Here's some money." He wanted to own it. Between us we gave that LP a run for the money. He played it on the weekends. Loud. And I played it every morning before going to school. Loud.

I worshiped Jack Teagarden. But when I played the trombone I sounded more like a poor man's Turk Murphy. I couldn't help it. I practiced hard; I tried to learn better technique. I could whistle or hum every Teagarden solo, note for note, sound every last trill, no matter how intricate. But when I blew into the trombone it was all so much huffing and puffing and the sound came out all rough and ragged, like an amateurish Turk Murphy.

But when Russ Longstreth and "Pook" Ellis, two talented high school musicians, formed a Dixieland band in the fall of 1955, they took me in on trombone because I knew most of the standard tunes. In spite of lessons with accomplished trombone players in the city, I made a hash out of trying to read music. But that didn't matter; jazz musicians didn't need sheet music. They played by ear, and I could do that, though I don't know why. Tell me the key, Russ, run through it once on the piano, and I can play it. That's why they accepted me— that and because they couldn't find anyone else.

We were lucky. Russ, a remembering fool, could play anything—anything he'd ever heard or you could whistle or hum. On his best nights, Pook's trumpet was a pretty fair imitation of the velvety sound of Bobby Hackett. "Buff" Cobb, star running back on the varsity gridiron and first clarinetist in the high school band, said he loved Dixieland, and wanted to be in the group.

So did big Ronnie Haggard. Ronnie was huge, all muscle and a smile that said I love life—so don't even think of messing it up for me. On the gridiron he was a fearless freight train of a fullback. Turned out he picked a good banjo. And if we got any dances to play Ronnie would scare away any bullies who thought they just might show off in front of their girlfriends by harassing the band.

We were, we announced with a flourish, the Bowery Boys Original Dixieland Jazz Band, but you can just call us the Bowery Boys. We took our name from the Bowery, a beer joint over on Ninth Street, the one right next door to Tommy Manzo's house. Tommy, our drummer, said we could rehearse there any afternoon. The joint featured a country and western band two or three nights a week and the drummer left his set up.

We were in like Flynn. The Bowery Boys set up shop on the bandstand many afternoons and worked and reworked old standbys like "Ja Da" and "Royal Garden

My trombone had more shine than I did.

Blues" and "Mabel's Dream," which for some time sounded more like "Mabel's Nightmare." At first we called our sessions "rehearsals." No, we weren't up there with Bix Beiderbecke's high school Wolverines, but we weren't half bad. We played with great spirit, loving every note of the music Louis Armstrong was popularizing. From our first session on, some of the bleary-eyed veterans of the barstools began applauding at the end of a number and asking could we play, say, "Bye, Bye Blackbird" or "Do You Know What It Means to Miss New Orleans?"

"There's a fifty-cent piece in it for you if you guys can

The Bowery Boys Jazz Band was available for concerts and dances.

play that song." Could we play it? We had Russ, remember. And those he wasn't sure he knew, he needed only to hear someone hum a few bars of and he was off, his fingers tickling the keys and his head bent down as close to the ivories as he could get. He said that was the way he felt the music. After hearing a chorus on the piano Pook and Buff played it like they had known it all their lives. I honked along on trombone. Our rehearsals turned into rousing jam sessions—almost as much fun as playing baseball.

We put out the word that the Bowery Boys Original Dixieland Jazz Band was available for concerts and dances. We told our friends to spread the news at their churches or YMCAs. We mailed out a flier to student government leaders at other schools. We promised happy music. Music you could dance to. Music that would make you want to dance. We didn't play "Fidgety Feet" for nothing.

No, we played it and scores of other numbers for money. We charged seventy-five to a hundred dollars for two or three hours of nonstop swinging jazz, old-style Dixie tunes, songs like "Five Foot Two, Eyes of Blue," toe-tapping music that's good for you. And the invitations to play rolled in. We played early Friday afternoon junior high "mixers" and "sock hops." You pay, we play. Senior high kids at other schools in the city hired us to liven up their "Teen Town"—where someone was always promising to do the "dirty boogie" but seldom did. We even got our share of Saturday night dances, even formal affairs. Want to do the Charleston? No sweat. Feel the romantic urge to dance cheek to cheek? No big deal. We could do "Blue Moon" or "Bye, Bye Blackbird" fast or slow. We play, you dance.

We would have played for nothing, but it was sweet picking up an extra fifteen or twenty bucks on a Friday, and sometimes a few more simoleons for a Saturday gig as well. It wasn't long before I was rolling in dough. There was no need to tell the folks, particularly Mom, who didn't mind doling out my hefty allowance. There was every reason not to tell her: she frowned mightily on dancing. Dancing was sinful. (Dancing leads to, well, you know what.) Playing in a dance band and leading others astray was just as bad as dancing. Maybe worse. Of course, that much moola, sometimes up to thirty or forty smackers a weekend, would have made Mom's fingers itch. But righteousness would have won out in the end. Sin was sin, no matter how you sliced it—or how much money it put in your pocket.

It was a breeze keeping it a secret from the folks. On Friday afternoons I would leave school with my trombone in the trunk of my '49 cruisin' Chevy. Once home, I announced that I had a date ("yes, a date; no, Mom, you don't know her") and would be shoving off soon. The date idea was great: it allowed me to leave the house decked out in the Bowery Boys uniform: gray slacks, red tie, white shirt, and blue blazer.

My deception, however necessary, had one drawback, one that didn't bother me much at all at the time. I never had a chance to play for my father. Would he have liked what he heard? Hard to say. I wouldn't bet on it. His finely tuned ear might have caused him to wince at some of my bumptious solos. And his incorrigible impulse to tell the truth, no matter how hurtful, might have brought words I didn't want to hear. But maybe he would have been pleased, even a little bit proud, that his oafish son not only loved the music but could also play it, if only after a fashion. I'd like to think so.

If only he could have been a fly on the wall the Saturday afternoon we played a wedding reception in Little Italy. A friend at school had convinced a member of his family to hire us. We arrived early to case the place. The piano was okay. Good. We were to set up on the stage at one end of a rather long, narrow hall. The place was all but deserted, but the wedding party and guests would be along in a while. Great. We were in the mood to play, and we had several new numbers we wanted to run through as we warmed up.

When the guests started to filter in we were told the

bride and groom were on their way and could we greet them with "Here Comes the Bride." Sure could. When the smiling newlyweds walked in arm in arm we played a restrained rendition of the song with just a hint of swing. The happy couple danced around the room. The priest, the parents, the members of the wedding, old people, young kids gathered around beaming. Then they joined in as the father of the bride and then various handsome Italian guys took a turn around the floor with the bride on their arm.

All through the piece the Bowery Boys were as solemn as deacons. Pook played a beautiful horn. Buff did several lyrical, low-register versions, always sticking close to the melody. The Bowery Boys Original Dixieland Jazz Band showed great restraint and did not segue into a swinging two-beat, jazzed-up version. When we finally brought the dreamy number to an end the audience clapped and stomped.

They loved us. This was going to be great.

We graciously acknowledged the approval and introduced the members of the band. More applause. Then we broke into a swinging, half-fast, danceable version of "Oh, You Must Have Been a Beautiful Baby," complete with a vocal aimed at the bride. The newlyweds beamed. But nobody danced. When we finished a few people applauded politely.

We announced our next song, saying that it contained some words of wisdom for all of us, particularly given the happy occasion. We then lit into a fox-trot rendition of "A Good Man Is Hard to Find." No one danced.

We glanced uneasily at each other. We'd never had this happen before.

Then a stooped, short, plump Italian lady, her long

black dress and shiny black hair highlighted by the showy white orchid pinned to her shoulder, came up to the foot of the stage. She motioned for Russ to bend over. "Can you guys play a polka?"

Sure can, ma'am. A big grin graced Russ's face when he looked up at the rest of us and said, let's do "Beer Barrel Polka." He'd lead off with a piano chorus or two and then we were to chime in. Let her rip.

We did. The Bowery Boys had never played "Beer Barrel Polka" before—or any polka for that matter—but we had a good time knocking it out. The dance floor jumped for joy. Everyone danced up a storm. The bride and groom hopped around the room. Little girls in white dresses danced with their daddies in their black suits; grandmas danced with grandpas; teenage sisters and female cousins hopped around the room. The priest polkaed with the little old lady in black. The joint was jumping. At the end of the number the room rocked with applause.

Better let the hall cool down a second. We launched into a slow, romantic number. We sounded cool. But only a couple or two danced. And at the end of the tune—scattered, tepid applause. Well, maybe it was time to heat the hall again. We cooked. Nobody danced. Nobody. Nobody applauded. Nobody.

Back came the little old lady in black. She motioned for Russ to listen and said, "Do you guys know any other polkas?"

Sure do, ma'am. We love polkas.

We do? Hadn't "Beer Barrel Polka" exhausted our repertoire of Polish delights?

Russ grinned. He put his head down near the keys for a few seconds, looked up, and asked mischievously whether any of us knew "Wedding Day Polka." Listen to a few bars and then jump in when you remember it. Russ's tune sounded vaguely like something I'd heard before, but I couldn't place it, and I knew it wasn't called "Wedding Day Polka." But it sounded like a polka and we joined in. Everybody danced. The revelers loved it. Thunderous applause.

After that we took turns thinking up new polkas, though several sounded suspiciously like "Beer Barrel Polka." But our audience seemed not to mind. Many had gotten heavily into the beer and wine and harder stuff.

After two hours or so of polkacising we packed our instruments away. The little old lady approached with a broad smile, paid us, and introduced us to a couple of guests who enjoyed our music so much they might just call us sometime. Yeah, I think the old man would have enjoyed the whole thing.

He would have liked even more, I think, the night we played for a party of Veterans of Foreign Wars, on Main Street, not far from the Country Club Plaza and the Ivanhoe Temple where the debate on the One Man Pastor System had stirred the believers.

We arrived early to set up. The piano was in tune, but just barely. The acoustics were pretty good. The room was loose. The VFW guys and their women had already gotten into the drink. Good. Adults were a lot easier to play for, we'd discovered, if they were a little tipsy.

They liked our music; they cut a rug to the hot numbers. But to give them a chance to cool down we iced the room every so often by playing a slow drag number, something really soulful like "Stars Fell on Alabama" or "I Can't Get Started with You."

To our delight, our happy, pie-eyed veterans of foreign

wars dug into their pockets to "feed the kitty"—a glass bowl sitting on top of my trombone case prominently placed in front of the band. We had perfected the art of persuading people to feed our hungry kitty. When someone came up between numbers with a request for a certain song, we looked at each other quizzically, glanced at "the kitty," and asked around the band, "Does anybody know this song?" A dollar or some significant change flipped into the bowl reminded us quickly of the song, and yes, we could play it. Thank you, thank you very much.

To clue everybody in, we put a couple of bucks in the bowl before we played a single note. On a good night the kitty brought in anywhere from ten to twenty bucks—enough for hamburgers and Cokes after we'd finished playing. The vets got the idea early on and fed the kitty generously.

Near the end of our last set a miracle happened. A tubby, florid VFW man with various medals on his suit jacket wobbled over between numbers and asked whether we could play "When the Saints Go Marching In." Not that! We'd come to hate that piece and had taken, almost as a matter of pride, to refusing to play it unless we felt we had no alternative—or someone fed the kitty some green. We shrugged our shoulders, mumbled that we weren't sure everybody in the band knew it. The war hero held up his hand as though to say hush, reached in his pocket with the other hand, and pulled out a wad of bills. He plunked a wad in the kitty.

Who were we to refuse this decorated war hero, a gentleman with such nice manners? This flashed through our collective consciousness when we noticed several twenty-dollar bills in that collection of greens he'd slipped our way. Yes, sir! We could get those saints marching down South Rampart Street. We were struttin' with some barbecue just thinking about that fat kitty.

We roared into "When the Saints Go Marching In." But our eyes were on that kitty. Quick. Get that stash of cash out before he sobers up and comes back for his money. I grabbed the kitty, crouched down behind the piano, and counted our windfall. Sixty, seventy, eighty, ninety, one hundred, one hundred and twenty bucks— there it was in slightly sweaty ten- and twenty-dollar bills. Let's see, add that to the twenty or so singles and the loose change in the kitty and the hundred and twenty smackers we were to make for playing—why, we had a pot of gold. Double cheeseburgers, extra fries, large Cokes tonight—no, make that milk shakes! We were filthy rich.

But we weren't. We were dumb. Only as we put our instruments away and watched the bleary, weary veterans depart the dance floor did it dawn on us. That fat bastard who'd dropped the money in the bowl was paying us. How stupid could you get. We trudged out into the night cursing the vets and all their kin. That fat son of a bitch had cheated us out of a small fortune.

God, how the old man would have enjoyed the whole gaudy spectacle. He would have taunted me forever about the night we got greedy. Had Mom been there, or learned about it, her mind would have lingered a split second on that nice, tidy sum of money—then she would have blistered my ear not about the sin of greed, but about having spent my time with dancers and drinkers. All in all, it's best we lived in our separate worlds.

13

"They Play Nine Innings in
the Big Leagues"

What did he know, that grumpy old man sitting there alone in the upper deck? We knew baseball. He didn't. He was just a chubby man with a beer and a beer belly, chewing languidly on a half-smoked cigar. He was watching the game from the upper deck, the same as we were; he wasn't down in the expensive box seats along the baselines by the dugouts. We would be out there on the field someday playing pepper, running wind sprints, taking batting practice. And it wouldn't be all that far in the future, either. Gino Costanza, Shortcake Durham, and I were sixteen and knew when a ball game was in the bag.

It was spring. April 1955. Old Blues Stadium had been rechristened Municipal Stadium and was now, at least to Kansas Citians, a thing of beauty with a brand new upper deck and a face-lift. And a brand-spanking-new scoreboard; well, almost new: it was a discard from the old Boston Braves, who'd deserted Beantown for Milwaukee two years earlier, but it was "plenty good enough," as my mother would say. Anyway, out there in the heartland, in Kansas City, few of us had ever seen a real major-league park before. The freshly painted green seats glistened. So did the green outfield fence; painted over now were the old gaudy advertisements like "Hit This Sign and Win a Helzberg Diamond Ring." That was minor-league stuff, bush-league stuff, strictly from hunger. The Blues were no more; long live the Kansas City Athletics.

Kansas City now had a major-league team, the former Philadelphia Athletics. So what if the A's had become the doormat of the American League, had finished an ignominious last in 1954; they were the team of the legendary Cornelius McGillicuddy. Now old Connie Mack's forlorn Athletics, thanks to one Arnold Johnson, had been sold and moved to Kansas City.

Opening Day, April 13, had been a sellout, with an overflow crowd close to thirty-three thousand strong. Harry Truman, who said Bess was the real fan in the family, threw out the first ball. Hopalong Cassidy and his wife sat grandly in the owner's box seats and smiled and waved to the admiring throng. Next to them sat "Home Run" Baker and the real home run hitter, Jimmie Foxx, legendary stars who'd played for old Connie Mack. H. Roe Bartle, the mayor, a huge, beefy man with leather lungs, was on hand. So great was his bellowing voice that he often grandly dismissed public-address systems and simply roared out at the crowd.

A giant procession, every bit as big as the annual American Royal parade, had snaked down Main Street to welcome our new gladiators. Let the smart alecks talk; let the cynics sneer that our A's were a washed-up, over-the-hill, sore-armed bunch. The *Star*'s longtime sportswriter,

Joe McGuff, said the A's would be lucky to finish sixth. The kids on Thompson Street knew better than that! We pointed with swelling admiration to Gus Zernial, a mountain of a man; "Ozark Ike," the writers dubbed him. "Man Mountain Dean," we called him in awe and reverence. So what if Big Gus was slow and heavy-footed in left field, check out his home-run swing. We idolized little Bobby Shantz. Robert Clayton Shantz, the pint-size southpaw, the pride of Pottstown, Pa., would regain his glory days. We just knew it.

Opening Day had been on Tuesday, a school day. There was no chance of getting tickets or ditching school and going to the game. The season began on a dizzying note of hope and faith—and sweet victory. Ewell "the Whip" Blackwell had ambled in from the bull pen in the late innings to nail down the victory over the Detroit Tigers. Was the Whip washed up? Was that the reason the Yankees had just sold him to Kansas City? Couldn't be. Wasn't his sidearm, "buggy-whip" delivery as wicked as it had ever been? You bet your life. The A's were fantastic, "premium." We had a big-league team. What a wonderful life.

The cavernous movie palaces downtown featured *Battle Cry* with Van Heflin; *On the Waterfront* with Marlon Brando; *The Caine Mutiny* with Humphrey Bogart. Grace Kelly was starring in *The Country Girl* with the crooner, Bing Crosby; Spencer Tracy was cool in *Bad Day at Black Rock.* Pious grownups, or Youth for Christ zealots, flocked to see *A Man Called Peter.*

The devil's crowd howled approvingly when Lili St. Cyr opened at the Folly Burlesque with her *Varietease.* The really hot news was that the new James Dean movie, *East of Eden,* was cool. It wasn't *Rebel without a Cause,* but Dean was Dean. Newscasters announced that Jonas Salk's miraculous polio vaccine had just become available to the public. Life was great.

The A's weren't. Not in the second game of the young season. The Tigers mauled them, 10–2. Arnold Portocarrero, a can't-miss lefty, a heartthrob to the girls and young women, got bombed. The day was cold and gray; only twenty thousand or so fans showed up. OK, so Kansas City was a cow town, a working-class town where not everybody could go to daytime ball games.

The A's went to Chicago, and it was the same old story—hard-luck Bobby Shantz pitched well but lost to the White Sox. The rains came and washed out games. The A's moved on to Detroit, where they dropped two, embarrassed, in one game, 16–0. Portocarrero was complaining of a stiff shoulder and a sore arm. Joe DeMaestri—the A's good field, no-hit shortstop—was injured. But he was our "Joe D." Gus hadn't hit a homer yet.

Across the border in Nebraska at the state university seven undergraduates were suspended for participating in a "panty raid." The silliness spread like cancer, eating away at morality at the University of Kansas and at Mizzou in Columbia. Church leaders and the respectable folks, the sort who wrote letters to the *Kansas City Star*, feared an epidemic of panty raids and, worse, "petting" among teenagers. The same sort of folks fretted with Billy Graham about that dreadful man Kinsey and his sex studies.

Ike worried that, compared to the leaner, tougher, hardened Europeans, America's youth were becoming "soft" and flabby. In comparative tests of "flexibility" and "muscular strength," American kids had failed big time. This was not good.

Just how bad, we didn't know. In some distant unheard of place called Vietnam—where did you say it was, near Korea?—American "advisers" had gone in to direct a civil war to its proper conclusion—the defeat of international communism in Asia. "Clash in Saigon" went the headline in the *Kansas City Star* that April day the paper reported panty raids and epidemics of petting. Ike said he'd have to have some $3.5 million from Congress to "meet the immediate threats to world security and stability now centered in Asia." Give it to him.

Was anybody in Kansas City listening, or worried? Folks out in the south part of town near the plaza— where houses cost more than the old man would ever see—might be concerned about some place called Saigon, but few in Northeast could pronounce let alone spell *Vietnam.*

The sun was shining in Kansas City and the A's were coming back for a home stand on April 18, a day of bloodshed in Saigon. Five thousand of the faithful greeted the A's plane at the city's already unsafe downtown airport. The Cleveland Indians were in town: Vic Wertz and Larry Doby and the rest of the giant-killers who'd dethroned my Yankees in 1954. They'd won 111 games, set a record, then dropped four straight to Willie Mays and the New York Giants in the World Series. You never know what's going to happen in baseball.

In addition to Wynn, Lemon, Feller, and Garcia, all ace right-handers, the Indians had Herb Score, a lefty, with a fast ball equal to Feller's in his prime. I had seen Score handcuff the Blues the previous year; he'd been the rookie sensation of the Indianapolis Indians. Mike "the Bear" Garcia would pitch the opening game of the series, and Score would be on the mound the next day.

Shortcake, Gino, and I weren't about to miss this game, which the scribes hyped as the "second opening day." It was a night game; we could go right after supper and arrive at the ballpark in time to watch batting practice. The sportswriters and city boosters had predicted a large crowd; fans were already lined up when we arrived just shortly after the gates opened.

Major leaguers rose to awesome heights of glory in batting practice. Big Gus, Bill Renna, Jim Finigan, Vic Power, and Kansas City's other sluggers hit screaming line drives and home runs. Larry Doby dazzled the multitude by smacking ball after ball over the right-field fence. These guys pounded the ball, bruised it. Their line drives screeched. No one hit lazy, looping fly balls, the sort we were coming to deride as "American Legion home runs."

We knew a lot in those days, almost everything. Still, we watched carefully, making mental notes on how the big guys stood at the plate, how they held the bat. When they fouled off a fat pitch they unleashed a stream of choice obscenities. Big-league cussin'.

Third basemen fired line drives of their own across the infield to the first basemen. Smack. Not even our keen eyes could detect the slightest hint of a loop in those pegs around the infield. Smack. Heavenly sound. The Blues had been good, but these guys were gods.

Did the A's have a chance? You damn betchie. Managing the team was Lou Boudreau, the former "boy wonder." Boudreau had picked Alex Kellner, one of the hometown heroes, to be on the mound for the A's.

Kellner set the Indians down in the first. Kansas City nicked the Bear for a run in the first. In the third, the heavens opened. Kellner—Lefty the pitcher—tripled!

Then the A's hit back-to-back home runs. One out later Big Gus broke out of his slump with a mighty blast. Behind the wall, little kids scurried to grab the ball, to lay their hands on a piece of history. More runs came in. The Bear trudged to the showers; the A's were up 7–0 after four. This game was in the bag.

Gino—nicknamed for the Dodgers' journeyman outfielder Gino Cimoli—and I started horsing around. We lost interest in keeping score, in marking balls and strikes and who hit what and where. The way the A's were hitting you might be penciling in something and miss a herculean blast. We threw our pencils, those stubby ones that came with the program, at each other. We yelled. We hollered stupid things at the Indian batters. We ate hot dogs and peanuts and wadded up the wrappers to throw down on the fans in the lower deck. We hit each other. An usher, an old man in a new but ill-fitting uniform, warned us to pipe down.

"Hey, you kids. Knock it off," growled the old-timer in the next row. "There's a ball game going on, for Chrissake."

We'd been snickering about that half-chewed cigar dangling from his lips. The temperature had dropped a bit, but there he sat in his sleeveless white cotton undershirt, his shirt wadded up under his seat. He wore an old Blues baseball cap; a patchy stubble marred his chin. *He* was keeping score.

"Take it easy, old-timer," I yelled back at him. "This game's in the bag."

"This game ain't over, buddy," he shot back. "Look at the scoreboard. There's a lot more baseball to be played. A lot can happen in five innings."

We jeered back at him and shouted something

insulting about that stogie, and how didn't he know smoking was bad for his health, and that cigars would cut down on his wind.

"Hey, they play nine innings in the big leagues, boys. You'd better learn that."

Who'd he think he was talking to? We guessed he must have had in mind that the second games of doubleheaders in the American Association, the Blues' old league, had been only seven innings. Yeah, who did he think he was talking to? Sure, major leaguers played nine innings. But this game was in the bag. Rack up another win, number two, for the new pepped-up Kansas City Athletics. We shoved off and made our way down to the lower deck in hopes of finding some unoccupied box seats.

The heavens fell. Cleveland scored five runs in the top of the fifth. Kellner went to the showers. The faithful groaned. The Indians scored two more in the seventh. KC got one back after the seventh-inning stretch and a rousing, rocking, hometown version of "Take Me Out to the Ball Game." We were spurring our boys to hold on. With two innings to go KC led 9–7.

The Indians got another run in the eighth. Now it was down to one inning. Cleveland, trailing by one, had three outs. Could they pull this one out? No way. This we knew for certain when in from the bull pen strolled the mighty Ewell Blackwell. The Whip could do it. The Indians had the bottom of the order up.

Old Ewell looked good. He was a tall—the scorecard said six foot five—menacing, right-handed sidearmer, lean and lanky, all bony arms and elbows and long legs with a beak of a nose perched on a chiseled face. Right-handed hitters hated it when he dipped low and flew—

all arms and legs—toward third base and buggy-whipped a fast ball toward their head or knees. In his prime, only the bravest of batters had held their ground when the Whip uncorked one of his slicing curve balls. Old Ewell had a reputation for being totally fearless and willing to brush any batter off the plate—the sort, like the Indians' grisly Early Wynn, who'd bragged that he would throw at his own mother "if she had a bat in her hand."

Oh, we knew that Blackwell was past his prime. But his magnificent glory days pranced before our eyes. Mr. Jim had seen to it that we knew baseball. "Who was the only pitcher to throw two consecutive no-hitters?" Johnny Vander Meer. "Who was the only pitcher to even come close to tying that record?" Ewell Blackwell, in 1947, the year the Whip won sixteen straight over one stretch.

Sadly, the Whip never marched such paths of sunlit glory again. After 1947 he had kicked around with a number of teams. He'd actually started a World Series game for the Yankees in the early 1950s, a game I'd listened to on the radio. Now he was with the lowly A's. Terror stalked our hearts.

But he'd held the lead on opening day. Maybe he could ice this game. We asked God for that. That didn't seem too much to ask. Thirty thousand fans at the ballpark prayed, beseeching God for one small favor. Just three more outs was the great silent prayer coming up from fans glued to their radios listening to Larry Ray. In Columbia, Excelsior Springs, Knob Noster, and Lexington the faithful prayed. So, too, did the loyal hopefuls in Napoleon, Wellington, and Waterloo and in Bolivar, St. Joseph, Peculiar, and Lone Jack—or any Missouri town where the radio would pick up the ball game.

The Whip walked the first batter. He hit the next one. Trouble. Then the old master regained his form. He fanned the next hitter and got a pop-up from a dangerous hitter, but only after he'd scorched a shot down the line, foul by a foot. Near panic.

Two outs, two on, a one-run lead. The batter: Larry Doby, the black star who'd integrated the American League a few months after Jackie Robinson changed the game forever. Doby's swing was a thing of beauty. Those towering shots he'd hit in practice now flashed ominously across the collective memory of everyone at the ballpark. Mr. Jim would be glued to his radio.

The Whip feared no man. Fans screamed for a reliever, a lefty to face the left-handed slugger. Sound baseball logic. But no. Boudreau, the Boy Wonder, decided the Whip would stay.

He tiptoed around disaster. He ran the count full. With two outs, those runners on first and second would be running on the pitch. A long single would give the Indians the lead. The Whip, deep in the shadow of his glory days, had lost more than a little off his fast ball. Now he needed every bit of cunning, savvy, guile still in his arm and head.

Blackwell pitched. The runners took off. Doby swung. A mighty swing. Smack. Silence. Time stopped. All eyes watched mournfully as the ball climbed heavenward. How long did it stay up there? Not long enough. When the ball flashed from the sky it landed well beyond the right-field fence. Thirty thousand true-blue fans stood in shock. When the mighty Doby touched home plate the Indians led 11–9.

But it ain't over till it's over. The A's had one last at bat. But hope was ebbing, vanishing swiftly into the cool spring night. The hometown heroes had outhit the Indians and clouted five home runs—to the Indians' one. But Doby's blast had washed all that away in the twinkling of an eye. Any lingering, never-say-die hope left on that April evening in 1955 was extinguished when Bob Feller came on to pitch the last inning. Why did they have to bring *him* in?

Our strong, mighty men were due up—Big Gus, Bill Renna. But down they went. They were overmatched. No one in Kansas City would hear tunes of glory tonight. The A's had won every inning but the last one, the one that counted. All those runs: nine of them, enough to win most ball games. All those hits and home runs. All for nothing.

The next day the scribes and bleacher bums and youngsters and old-timers at the countless bars and barbershops and front porches of Kansas City tried to put the best face on it all. Our Blues—no, our A's—had given it their all, given the fans their money's worth. Nothing to be ashamed of. Five home runs. Nine runs. Like springtime flowers these were sure signs that better days were ahead. It was only April.

The season was young. There were lots more games to play. No one, going in, really believed that Big Gus, Bobby Shantz, Jim Finigan, Arnie Portocarrero, and the Whip would win any pennants. But I would have given the world for a win that night. Turns out, that old man with the beer and the half-chewed stogie knew what he was talking about. They do play nine innings in the big leagues.

14

"Take Your Hands Off Them Boys"

I t was, we quickly learned that summer of 1955, wondrously easy to sneak into Municipal Stadium to watch the A's play. Sneaking in allowed us to enjoy the games with a sense of sweet satisfaction that we had triumphed over some nameless, faceless enemy. All we had to do was go around by the side of the stadium, just up the way from the ticket gates behind home plate, and scale a chain-link fence. It was a high fence, ten or twelve feet, and one that deterred the honest, the aged, the greatly overweight, the moral, and the virtuous. We were none of those things.

We could hardly plead poverty. We had the jack to pay for cheap bleacher tickets. All of us had paper routes or jobs sacking groceries down at Chernikoff's or Milgrim's, the local food-store chain. I always had money in my pockets in those days. On Friday evenings after coming home from work my mother gave me $15.00. That was my "allowance," and it was to cover my lunches for the upcoming week and a meal for that evening. "I never feel like cooking on Fridays," she announced wearily each week, "so go get yourself a hamburger or something."

That $15.00 was a very interesting sum in those days. It more than covered my Friday night meal, my lunches, gasoline for my nifty Chevy. I didn't feel it would be right for me to question her generous evaluation of my financial needs. Nor did I tell her that on many weekends I was picking up another twenty bucks or more playing trombone with the Bowery Boys Original Dixieland Jazz Band. On many weekends I had a fat billfold; I was "deep in pocket," as Mr. Jim would say.

Sneaking into the ballpark became part of the ritual of going to the games. We took the bus, or hitched a ride with someone going to the game. If we rode the bus, we walked unafraid, and sometimes stridently, through several blocks of the black section surrounding the stadium at Twenty-second and Brooklyn. But so great was the unseen wall between white Northeast and Kansas City's blacks that we never once thought of going to see the Kansas City Monarchs, kings of the old Negro leagues. When the Blues and then the A's were away, the Monarchs played in the white owner's stadium, but I knew no one who even knew anything about the black team, let alone went to their games. What a loss—for us. But for that invisible but granite wall of racism and unthinking indifference, we would have seen Ernie Banks, Kansas City's own Satchel Paige, and others, including the legendary "Buck" O'Neil, the Monarchs' manager. What knuckleheads we were.

Once inside to see the A's, we made straight for the bleachers. There, the ushers didn't bother checking for tickets. Midway through the game, we made our way down to the box-seat sections. We were looking for unoccupied seats, good seats that companies or organizations had bought for the season, mainly to give away to clients or to the Scouts or some other worthy organization. Some of the choicest seats were almost always vacant. As the season wore on and the A's continued to lose and the fickle fans lost their initial enthusiasm, we became quite adept at finding whole groups of vacant seats.

Many of the ushers were tolerant and looked the other way when we sat down in seats that were obviously not for the likes of us. By the fourth or fifth inning, we were usually safe from even the most zealous officials. By that time, it was obvious that the rightful ticket holders weren't going to show up and there'd be no tips for escorting them and making an elaborate gesture of wiping off the seats. On hot afternoons or evenings, as the losing games wore on, the ushers tended to retire to the back of the park to sneak a beer or slip out and go home early. We were left free to enjoy the game like kings on our thrones.

Occasionally overzealous ushers harassed us and demanded to see our tickets. We protested that we had bought tickets but had pitched the stubs aside earlier. Or we put on an elaborate show of searching our pockets and billfolds, swearing that we had just had them and had shown them to that other guy up the aisle. Some of the ushers took a fiendish delight in scowling and gesturing that we'd have to "get out" and that they'd throw us out of the ballpark if they ever caught us sneaking around again.

Then one day some security guards got wind of the fact that we had no tickets at all. Soon they discovered not only that we were sneaking in, but where. The stadium authorities planted a guard to stand near the fence. But he wasn't always on duty, so we continued to climb over and make our way to the bleachers.

When he was around we worked out a plan to approach the fence stealthily and send one of our number ahead to ask him a question and seek directions. Then several of us would sprint to the fence, scale it quickly, and run like the devil, scattering in all directions. When the hapless guard gave chase, our decoy scout and any others with him would climb the fence and head for our agreed-upon rendezvous spot.

We greatly enjoyed the game of wits with the guard, the running away, and the danger—though we were never in much real peril of being caught by the old or fat security guards. We were young, in shape, fleet of foot. I was the slowest of our group, but even I could outrun our pursuer.

On occasion, when the game was dull or we were about ready to leave and go do something else, we would actually walk around near where we knew the guard sat and get just close enough for him to recognize us. Then we would take off in a sprint and leave the stadium.

It was all so easy. It was all great fun. We had mastered various tricks of sneaking in and enjoying free entertainment. Getting into movie theaters was easy—one or two of us would buy tickets and creep to the exit, open the door, and let our buddies in. Drive-in movies presented another welcome challenge to our ingenuity—several of us would cram ourselves into the trunk while another could lie on the floor behind the front seat covered by a blanket or newspapers or a cardboard box or two. Getting caught was no big deal: the punishment was usually to be sent packing with a stern admonition about what would happen "if I ever catch you pulling this stunt again."

Sneaking out also offered charms. Our high school metal shop workroom opened conveniently onto the alley between the school building and the football field. After Mr. Sims announced, "All right, men, let's go to work," he made straight for his locked shed to fetch a valuable tool or a piece of metal reserved for someone with an actual interest in fashioning oversize metal fruit trays or large, ugly rings. With Mr. Sims in his shed, we ran into the alley and onto the football field. In English or history classes or wherever the entry door was in the back of the room, it was nothing to have someone go up to the teacher's desk and block the view. Then several of us slipped out of our chairs, got down on our hands and knees, and crawled to the back of the room and out the door. Freedom awaited.

No, sneaking in and out of theaters, classrooms, drive-in movies, and Municipal Stadium was no big deal. It was a breeze. Life was a game. Breaking the rules, and getting away with it, made the game all the sweeter.

Then disaster struck. We went to the ballpark and followed our foolproof plan. The security man was nowhere to be seen. We climbed the fence leisurely, those in front offering a helping hand to those coming over behind them. We sauntered off in the direction of the bleachers. Suddenly, a squadron of security guards swarmed around us. Several of us took off running. But Gino and I and a couple of others were trapped. We had nowhere to run.

We weren't all that afraid. We assumed we'd be bawled out and kicked out of the park and given an earful of dire warnings and threats about "next time." But this time our captors had a glint in their eye. Three or four of them corralled us, laid firm, reprimanding hands on our shoulders—"hey, man, take it easy"—and told us we were in big trouble. They'd had their eye on us for some time, they announced, barely able to conceal their glee, and now we were going to get what we deserved, "you troublemaking bastards." We were going to be delivered into the hands of the police, who would surely haul us downtown and have us arrested.

Our pleas for mercy—at first mocking, and then sincere—and for forgiveness went unheeded. Instead, our captors rebuked us with foul language about what we had coming to us. Our promises, quite heartfelt at that moment, to repent, to reform, and never, never sneak in again were also rudely rejected. We were told to shut up, that we were "in deep shit." I was scared, genuinely scared—of the police and of what the old man would say and do.

We started off toward our rendezvous with fate. As they led us toward our meeting with the police, the security guards squeezed our arms and shoulders. They'd been itching for this moment, and they were savoring it. As we walked along our guards grew even more profane and graphic about what the police would do to us and how we would "have a police record for the rest of our lives."

Walking toward us came three large men in dark pinstriped suits. They had on white shirts and ties and pinstriped vests that matched their suits. Their black shoes glistened. They were clean-shaven with thick, dark, oily hair. Each topped two hundred pounds, but they carried themselves with a nonchalant confidence. One was eating a bag of peanuts. They were utter strangers to me.

But as we drew nearer to them they eyed us closely. Their eyes fastened on Gino. They stopped. As we walked by them, they talked in low voices and gestured with their hands. One of them seemed to point at Gino. The swarthiest one clenched his fists, straightened himself up, pulled his shoulders back, and put his clinched hands to his hips, a look of utter disgust on his face as he stared at the security guards. Those three guys in their pinstriped suits didn't look like anyone you'd want to mess around with.

Our guards seemed to pay no attention to them, though they appeared to step up their pace just a bit as they pushed on toward what we had coming to us. We had not gone more than two or three steps past the three portly Italians when we heard one of them say, "Hey, take your hands off them boys." The words were sharp, distinct, clear; we had the exhilarating feeling that the man meant what he was saying. Our captors shoved us forward.

"I said take your hands off them boys," the voice rang out again.

Our captors stopped abruptly. One of them turned and said, "Who are you."

"Never mind who we are," said the man with his hands on his hips. "You take your hands off them boys."

Our guard who had taken the most delight in ordering us around replied that we had been caught breaking the law, sneaking into the ballpark. We'd even lipped off, when caught. And this wasn't the first time we'd climbed over the fence and refused to halt when pursued. "We're taking these boys to the police." We noticed that his voice seemed to have lost a bit of the swaggering arrogance. His tone now had a trace of deference. Or was it fear?

"I said take your hands off them boys. I'm not goin' to tell you again. I don't care how many times they broke into this fucking ballpark."

Then the slightly older man, the one in sunglasses, the one who had whispered something to one of his companions and seemed to point to Gino, reached into his pocket and pulled out a wad of bills. What a bundle of money, what a waddolla! It was, to our starstruck teenage eyes, a massive head of cabbage. He actually had a handful of one-hundred-dollar bills in his chubby paw.

"Box seats for these boys," he said in a very low, gravelly voice. It was a voice that could bring a chill down your spine—or a sense of elation, if you were on your way to the police station and a session with the old man.

But these boys are lawbreakers, one of the guards started to say. The man in the sunglasses slowly, deliberately, transferred the head of cabbage to his left hand and held up his right hand in a manner that demanded silence. The time for talking, at least by our captors, was over. Everyone felt it.

"I said box seats for these boys. The best box seats in the park."

Our guards relaxed their grips, took their hands off us. They began smiling meekly at the man in the sunglasses and saying, "Yes, sir" and "We'll be glad to, sir."

"You," said the man with the money as he peeled off a hundred-dollar bill. He pointed to the guard who had spoken to him. "You take this money, and buy these boys box seats, them extra good ones down by the A's dugout."

Our guard took the money meekly, but turned quickly on his heel and almost ran down the aisle to the ticket window. He was back in a flash with four box-seat tickets in one hand and change from the hundred-dollar bill in the other. His hand shook ever so slightly when he stretched out his arm to give the tickets and the change to the man in the sunglasses.

Whoever was behind those sunglasses was our savior, but he seemed more menacing than ever. With a wave of his hand he sent our former guards on their way. He then turned to us and gave us each a ticket. He also peeled off a ten-dollar bill for each one of us. Go enjoy the game, he said. We thanked him profusely, but his grim expression changed not at all and something inside told us to shut up. He and his friends turned and walked away, absorbed in some conversation we couldn't hear. We never saw any of them again.

15

"She's Gone About As Far As She Can Go"

I n the 1950s Kansas City's Northeast was hardly
a Babylon of forbidden joys, but sneaking into
ball games or movies, or swiping Old Man Pierce's
orange concentrate, or driving across town to jam with
the Bowery Boys and get paid for it to boot—well, these
were the wines of our youth. And no one drank them
more exuberantly than the charter members of the
Riding Around Gang.

The Riding Around Gang formed itself in 1955, soon
after the old man bought that Chevy beauty for me; it
was the year Gino, Dennis, Delmer, Ralph, and I reached
the magical age of sixteen and raced to get our driver's
licenses. We cruised Northeast's drive-ins doing our best
imitations of James Dean and told ourselves we were
looking for sex, for "loose women."

But what we really wanted was some young girl our
own age just to notice one of us. Our incessant talk about
girls and sex was just that—all talk. But we thought
about it all the time. At least I did. No, baseball, then sex.
And since the Riding Around Gang wasn't "getting any,"

our conversations were intense.

We were double dumb. This was about the time we started calling Ralph, he of the sandy hair and innocent expression, Ralphie Joe. And then for some idiotic reason we dubbed him "the Menopause Baby." What did that mean? How should we know? And how could we know that we had been struck stupid by adolescence? But the more Ralphie Joe fretted and demanded to know what a "Menopause Baby" was, the more we called him that, telling him only that we would tell him, someday, "when you are mature enough."

We pumped quarters into those "adult-only" peep show machines at the Penny Arcade, at the corner of Twelfth and Main. Our lust was rewarded with cheap, grainy films of big, peroxided blond, buxom women in black lingerie slithering around on round beds or huge couches for no apparent reason. When our money ran out, or we couldn't find any unsuspecting young girls on the street to ogle, I repeated the story of Big Red one more time.

We lived in constant expectation of "seeing something" in those "art films" shown at the Kimo Theater on Main Street, down the street from Jay McShann's legendary jazz bar. We were suckered by every advertisement and come-on from the Kimo's sexy posters, but always our hopes were dashed against the rocky shores of reality. Older boys bragged they had seen "the real thing" in dirty movies shown to old men at gatherings called "smokers." Now, *there* you see everything! But the closest we ever got was seeing Brigitte Bardot traipsing around in her underwear in the movie *And God Created Woman*. God had created woman, all right, but apparently not for our lustful eyes. "Tell us about Big Red!"

We saw more in 1955 when we discovered the Folly Burlesque Theater at Twelfth and Central. Respectable Kansas City, old cow town, didn't know whether to laugh or cry about the seedy striptease joint. With its gaudy flashing neon lights and posters of this week's star "dancers," the Folly Burlesque was a thoroughly disreputable eyesore.

Rogers and Hammerstein's *Oklahoma* had immortalized the Bur-le-que where "she went about as far as she could go." The ancient Follies was one of the reasons "Everything's Up to Date in Kansas City." Friday nights in the fall and winter of 1955 were hope-we-can-see-something time for the Riding Around Gang—if the Bowery Boys weren't playing or if one of us hadn't miraculously gotten a date. The Gang piled into my Chevy or Delmer's sleek black 1948 Mercury—hood and trunk neatly "leaded in" and the spitting image of James Dean's car in *Rebel without a Cause*—and headed straight for the Follies.

"Yes, I'm sixteen. What do you need, my driver's license?"

"Look, I have to be sure," answered the little old lady in the ticket cage out front. "Suppose I let you boys in and you're underage and the cops raid this place? What do you think'll happen to me if one of you boys ain't sixteen?" This she repeated week after week.

"No cops," we replied flippantly, "are gonna raid this flea-bitten firetrap. It smells like somebody mixed stale beer and horse piss!" That last part or some other obscenity we uttered only when out of earshot of the ticket lady or the "bouncer."

The theater was old, dark, and grungy. Many of the seats were broken. The carpet was threadbare. Drunks, derelicts, winos, used the place to sleep off binges. In winter the place provided a warm, temporary refuge from the freezing, unforgiving cold. The shows lasted two hours, starting at midday and running until midnight. Saturday night promised a special, brazenly "hot" late show, but midnight was our curfew, and we had to take a pass on the sure thing.

Once inside the palace of pleasure we plopped ourselves down for the early evening show. Even if we got there early we rarely got a seat down near or on the front row. Those seats usually went to those who had come during the earlier show and had stayed on for the next one, moving down to get a better seat when the crowd thinned out—a trick we soon learned.

Dancers and comedians direct from Las Vegas!

A small ragtag band was on hand in the pit with a little old lady on piano. She sat right below the stage with her back to the audience and her eyes fixed on the action above to know when to begin beating out a hot number. At the cry of "Show Time," the band ripped into a bump-and-grind song. The frayed burgundy curtain opened and the announcer exulted that tonight's show featured dancers and comedians "direct from Las Vegas." As the band lit into a lively tune a leggy dancer in a flowing dress and high heels pranced onto the stage, danced provocatively for a chorus or two, and then strutted her stuff with a tantalizing striptease. Week after week we waited expectantly, sometimes hardly able to breathe, for a vision of the promised land.

The dancers were of indeterminate age and came in all sizes and shapes. Some were beauties and goddesses. Some, the younger ones usually, threw themselves into their routines with smiles and a joy that seemed as genuine as our pent-up longings. These artistes we cheered with the gusto only randy sixteen-year-old boys could muster. We stomped and whistled and shouted to encourage our heart's darlings to forget the law and throw everything off.

So loud and so earnest were our encouragements that the little old lady at the piano would sometimes turn around and wink at us and yell, "Come on, take it off for the boys." Our favorite dancers gave us our money's worth by smiling and winking at us, tempting us to believe that they were going to heed our cries and "go all the way." They never did.

The baggy-pants comedians entertained with bawdy routines and one-liners that were probably as old as the hills. But the Riding Around Gang loved them. Their raunchy jokes could be repeated endlessly on the ball field or the street corner.

In time our infatuation with the Follies waned, and we devised new ways of misbehaving. We sat through a show and then amused ourselves by yelling out the punch lines to the comedians' jokes. We were cruisin' for a bruisin' and we knew it.

First would come the long, cold stare from the old hoofers onstage who'd heard everything. They walked slowly to the edge of the stage, peered down at us, and said, "What did you guys do, bring your lunch?"

When that didn't silence us they unleashed a barrage of one-liners: "Hey, I don't come to where you work and kick the broom, do I?" or "Don't get it out often, eh, boys?" or "Zip up your pants and go home." When we protested that it was hot or cold out there, they sneered, "Then don't leave it out there." The next face we saw was the ugly mug of the bouncer who told us to hit the bricks!

More fun, though, was our carefully orchestrated response at intermission when the announcer hawked boxes of candy the ushers offered for sale. "There's a valuable prize in each and every box."

We knew a true flimflam man when we saw one. Time for retaliation. About the time his rummy ushers were halfway up the aisle, one of us jumped up and shouted, "Hey, I got a ring, I got a ring!"

The barker could grit his teeth and smile. "These boys won! Who'll be next to buy a box of candy?"

"Hey, look here," one of us jumped up and shouted after a few delicious seconds had gone by, "can you believe it! I won a watch! A watch! Look at this baby." At that moment the rest of us examined the valuable gift and waved it in the air. The shyster onstage began signaling the bouncer to be ready.

We had the entire audience in our hand. We continued handing each other the phony watch and waving it triumphantly. We hadn't studied those masters in baggy pants for nothing. We knew precisely how long we could stretch (and savor) the dramatic pause before delivering the punch line.

"Hey, wait a minute! Something's wrong," we yelled. With a flourish one of us put the watch to his ear. Then we shouted angrily, "But the damned thing doesn't work!" With that the holder of the watch raised his arm in the air and threw the fake watch to the floor, shouting, "We want our money back. That watch is as phony as a two-dollar bill!"

That brought the burly bouncer running down the aisle, shouting, "Out, get out of here, you sons-a-bitches! Get out of here and don't come back!"

But we got our revenge. A month or so later we went back, got in, and walked hurriedly past the unsuspecting bouncer. We enjoyed the show. We laughed at the jokes, sang out lustily with the rest of the crowd, "take it off," and applauded grandly.

At intermission, when the pitchman was successfully selling candy, I jumped up and cried out, "I don't feel well! I'm sick. This crummy candy's rotten!" I groaned loudly, grabbed my stomach, bent over, and retched loudly.

We hurried up the aisle. I continued moaning and groaning, gasping for breath. Even old sleepy drunks recoiled and turned their heads away. "He's got to get some air," my pals yelled as we made for the lobby and out the door.

Such books and magazines were allowed in class, but Miss Brown drew the line at anyone reading a "dirty" book, which to her mind was virtually any paperback with a lurid cover, books like *God's Little Acre* or *Tobacco Road* or anything by that "filthy-minded man" Mickey Spillane. Anybody caught reading that trash in her class would be sent to the principal's office on the spot. She needn't have worried. Erskine Caldwell was a pop-up compared to Mark Harris.

One day I stumbled across a worn, dog-eared paperback dictionary in the hall. I picked it up and asked Gino and Ralphie Joe and several of my other buddies if they knew anyone who'd lost such a book. They said no, they didn't even know anybody who had one. I had no use for it, but I pitched it in my locker.

Several days later I was sitting in Miss Brown's study hall, a large section held in the school auditorium. It was the middle of the day. Nothing much had happened. Boredom, no stranger to anyone in study hall except the college bound, began to creep around the auditorium. Then a brilliant, beautiful idea came to me.

I arose from my seat, walked down to Miss Brown's desk, and asked her permission to go to the bathroom. She wasn't pleased with my request but said, "Don't be all day. Get back here and do some studying."

Yes, Miss Brown.

I dashed to my locker. I fished out that dictionary. I scrunched it under my arm so that old eagle-eye Brown with her extra-thick glasses that magnified her big round eyes would just barely be able to see it. As I sauntered by her desk, I cast a sheepish eye her way. When I reached my seat I slumped as far down as I could, opened my magazine, put my dictionary behind it, and pretended to

Once out on the street and halfway down the block we burst into uncontrollable laughter. Tears of victory and joy streamed down our faces. I held aloft the now empty can of Campbell's vegetable soup and tossed it jubilantly in the air.

Such, such were the joys of a misspent youth in Kansas City. If *she* didn't go about as far as she could go, we certainly tried to.

16

Being Idiots and Morons Together

The old man was right. Any idiot or moron could graduate from Northeast High School in the 1950s. In fact, if you picked your teachers carefully, selecting known softies, you could breeze through and never crack a book. Most of the teachers handed out passing grades routinely, requiring only that ignoramuses sit quietly in the back of the room and not pass notes around or make funny faces or snap chewing gum or always be bugging them for permission to go to the bathroom, where they assumed you were going to grab a quick smoke.

Yes, there were some teachers who demanded that you do some work, but not many. The Riding Around Gang avoided them. And yes, there were some serious students who wanted and received an education. They were the "college bound," girls mainly, nice girls who had a "good reputation" and wore long wool skirts and cashmere sweaters and bobby socks and penny loafers. The pretty *and* smart ones were the object of every boy's desires. I lusted after one myself. These young women sat in the

front row in every class. They actually br and books and notebooks and opened them class started, and took notes and held the and knew the answer when the teacher aske They made the teachers smile.

My friends and I, being idiots and moro made our teachers frown. Our antics sometin them to the edge of rage—or tears.

Rather than go straight to class, we milled the hall, in groups, like great herds of grazing b dutifully wore our school uniform: a plain wh and blue jeans neatly rolled up at the bottom and worn dangerously low on the hips, as low allowed. For moronic fun we liked to sneak up buddy and depants him, particularly if he was sweet-talk a young college-bound girl.

When the bell rang we dashed for the cl shoving each other to get into our seats, making commotion as possible, sometimes falling onto t We seemingly had forgotten how to walk or spea we still enjoyed hitting each other on the arm Miss Brown, he started it. Anyway, he ain't hurt.

"Just sit down and be quiet. That's all I ask o said our Miss Brown wearily. Once we quieted she was content to talk to the front-row girls and look our absorption in *Sport* magazine or Mark H baseball novels, *The Southpaw* and *Bang the Drum* two hardbacks we "borrowed" from the library and at least a half dozen times. We devoured the *Spo News,* the old-timey bible of baseball facts and fig and took an open-minded view of the upstart *S Illustrated,* born in 1955. But our heart's darling was the venerable *Sport* magazine.

read—and waited. It didn't take long.

"You, young man," she said, pointing an angry, snapping finger in my direction. "What book did you bring in here just now? What are you reading?"

"I'm just studying my book, Miss Brown," I said, looking up at her but keeping my dictionary out of sight. The room went silent.

"You come down here this moment," she fired back, "and bring that dirty book with you."

"Now, Miss Brown," I replied haltingly, "this isn't what you think. It's a book I need for English class." She knew good and well I was lying. When had I ever read anything for any English class? She was halfway convinced and partly right that English was a foreign language to me.

"You bring that book down here right now," she fired back, her voice rising. "Don't think you can pull the wool over my eyes. Come down here this instant!"

I arose slowly and ambled down the aisle, already savoring my coming triumph. I held the book behind me. When I arrived at her desk I hesitantly handed it to her, saying it was just something important I needed for a term paper.

She snatched the book from my hand, glanced at it, then looked at it solemnly. Fury reddened her face. Slowly she raised her eyes to meet mine. She stared at me for a long moment—those big eyes snapping—and then barked, "Get back to your seat."

Miss Brown was down, but was she down for the count? When I moseyed into her history class the next day she looked at me as if I were a communist or something. She said not a word, she just stared at me. I went to the back of the room, sat down, and opened a magazine and began reading. Class went on as usual: she talked to the girls on the front row and several college-bound boys who sat near the front. She uttered not a word to me or my buddies in the amen section. Several weeks went by and all remained quiet on the western front.

Then it was time for our six-week grade report and I braced for the tongue-lashing the old man would dish out when he saw my string of M's. At the end of the hour Miss Brown said she had our cards marked and ready for us to take on to our next class. But, she announced in a voice of ice water, she would like to see me for just a moment.

When I came to her desk she gave me the evil eye and held out my card but refused to let go of it. "I don't like the subpar level of your work," she said, prompting me to wonder what "work" she had in mind. "And I don't like your attitude." She was giving me a grade of I, she went on, and if I didn't shape up, would make that Inferior an F the next time, which just happened to be the grade report for the semester.

"Aren't you on the basketball team?" she asked, still clutching my grade card.

"Yes, ma'am," I told her. Something told me it was time to be extra polite.

Well, she knew that, though she didn't go to the games. She had more important things to do. But she'd talked to Coach Huhn, the same man who had flailed me with the towel several weeks back. He shared her view that I needed waking up, even failed, if she thought best. Thanks, Coach!

"So take this grade as a warning. Because should you get an F for this semester you'll be ineligible; you won't be playing any sports next term, and probably won't graduate, either, will you? You'll have to go to summer school." With that she plunged a dagger in my heart, and she knew it.

Don't go crying to Coach Huhn, I told myself. "Chalky" (given to chewing nervously on a piece of chalk during a tense game) was always going on about how he had no time for stupid ballplayers and how it was our responsibility to stay eligible to play. He wouldn't lift a finger to change Miss Brown's mind. He'd probably make me run extra laps after practice "so you can think about what your teacher told you."

I mumbled something to Miss Brown about doing better during the upcoming six weeks and walked away in a daze. Not be eligible? That was a fate worse than death, Gino and my teammates agreed. Just who does she think she is? She can't get away with that! Can she? Yup.

I hotfooted it to Miss Brown to ask what I needed to do to make amends, to get an M for the semester. She knew exactly what I needed to do. In addition to reading the textbook—oh, horror!—and coming to class prepared to say something, I was to copy out entries on American history from a fat encyclopedia in the school library. And I was to pick meaty pieces that pertained to what we were doing in class. "And not just a bunch of short entries, either," she snapped. I was to hand in three a week until she was satisfied with my attitude. Also, I was to sit on the front row. God Almighty, she knew how to get her pound of flesh. She was tougher than the old man at grade-card time, meaner than Old Man Pierce. I cursed that damned dictionary.

But I was sure the joke was on her. She excused me from study hall and told me to go to the library and start reading and copying the encyclopedia. I was pretty sure

I could goof off in the stacks with someone. But it turned out that Miss Brown had tipped off the librarian. I had to sit at a table near her desk.

But then something strange happened. After a while, I didn't mind thumbing through the encyclopedia, reading and copying out my weekly quota. Some entries bordered on being, well, almost interesting. Andrew Jackson, "Old Hickory," wasn't too bad; he was no Neat Guy. Neither was this lunatic John Brown. The old boy was crazy as a bedbug, but when they hanged him he didn't cry like a baby. Abraham Lincoln made for good reading, too, but I wasn't up to copying out his entire life. There was all that Civil War business.

But I was cool. I didn't utter a peep to any of my pals—some of whom volunteered to sit with me in the library—that some tiny part of me had come to enjoy, even look forward to, my daily sessions with the encyclopedia.

Then, midway through my incarceration in the library, heaven began to smile on me. One of the prettiest college-bound girls started coming in every day. Soon she began choosing a chair across the table from me. What's happening here? For most of the year, I had drooled just thinking about her. But she knew I was a clown. She was not only a knockout, she was a class officer, a wheel in the elite Literary Society—someone, said her admirers, so brainy she could "write her own ticket to any college." The book on her was that she had a lock on being valedictorian. So what's she doing sitting close to me?

I glanced up from my absorption in the encyclopedia and smiled at her. She smiled back. What was I doing, she wondered. Oh, studying. I tried to sound nonchalant. Did I come here every day at this time? Oh yes, I replied, I'm doing some special work for history. "It's my favorite class." (Don't push it, you big dummy!)

She liked history too, but English was her favorite. She liked to write poetry. Gee, me too. Well, I mean, I like reading it now and then. And I love English, too. I really like *Ivanhoe*. Did she? He's great, isn't he? Who, she said, Ivanhoe or Sir Walter Scott? Oh, both, both are really good. Who's my favorite character in the book, other than Ivanhoe? Well, now, that's a tough one to answer, there are so many great ones.

Was all this happening to me? Could this cute, pretty, popular, beautiful, sexy—she radiated loveliness in those cashmere sweaters—brainy, college-bound, valedictorian-in-the-making actually be sitting here whispering to me? Did it mean anything? She was probably taking pity on me. She was known to be really polite, even to idiots and morons. She probably knew that Miss Brown had banished me to the library.

I didn't know. But the next day I made sure to wear my letter sweater—the white one with the big purple N on the front—on the off chance I might shine some in her eyes. On the fourth or fifth day I screwed up my courage and asked her if she was doing anything that weekend and would she like to go see a movie and have a Coke and hamburger. She said yes. Thank you, thank you, thank you, God!

"What does she see in you, you big ape?" Ralphie Joe demanded to know.

"I don't know, but we're going on a date, a real date," I answered proudly.

It was the letter sweater that won her over. Or perhaps it was my reputation for being a class clown—they say

It was the letter sweater that won her over.

brainy, nice girls have a soft spot in their hearts for cutups. Perhaps her religious upbringing—her older brother was bound for the Baptist pulpit—propelled her to think she could reform me.

I didn't care what the reason was. I was in love. On the spot. In love. Years later she told it was my burr haircut. I didn't believe her. Still don't. (Whatever it was, we were married a few years later.)

At the end of the semester, just about the time writer's cramp was beginning to set in, Miss Brown said that she was satisfied with my work. No more bouts with the encyclopedia, "unless, of course, you want to." Well, now, I'll have to think about that. But she said sternly

Once out on the street and halfway down the block we burst into uncontrollable laughter. Tears of victory and joy streamed down our faces. I held aloft the now empty can of Campbell's vegetable soup and tossed it jubilantly in the air.

Such, such were the joys of a misspent youth in Kansas City. If *she* didn't go about as far as she could go, we certainly tried to.

16

Being Idiots and Morons Together

T he old man was right. Any idiot or moron could graduate from Northeast High School in the 1950s. In fact, if you picked your teachers carefully, selecting known softies, you could breeze through and never crack a book. Most of the teachers handed out passing grades routinely, requiring only that ignoramuses sit quietly in the back of the room and not pass notes around or make funny faces or snap chewing gum or always be bugging them for permission to go to the bathroom, where they assumed you were going to grab a quick smoke.

Yes, there were some teachers who demanded that you do some work, but not many. The Riding Around Gang avoided them. And yes, there were some serious students who wanted and received an education. They were the "college bound," girls mainly, nice girls who had a "good reputation" and wore long wool skirts and cashmere sweaters and bobby socks and penny loafers. The pretty *and* smart ones were the object of every boy's desires. I lusted after one myself. These young women sat in the front row in every class. They actually brought pencils and books and notebooks and opened them, even before class started, and took notes and held their hands up and knew the answer when the teacher asked a question. They made the teachers smile.

My friends and I, being idiots and morons together, made our teachers frown. Our antics sometimes brought them to the edge of rage—or tears.

Rather than go straight to class, we milled around in the hall, in groups, like great herds of grazing buffalo. We dutifully wore our school uniform: a plain white T-shirt and blue jeans neatly rolled up at the bottom of each leg and worn dangerously low on the hips, as low as the law allowed. For moronic fun we liked to sneak up behind a buddy and depants him, particularly if he was trying to sweet-talk a young college-bound girl.

When the bell rang we dashed for the classroom, shoving each other to get into our seats, making as much commotion as possible, sometimes falling onto the floor. We seemingly had forgotten how to walk or speak softly; we still enjoyed hitting each other on the arm. "Hey, Miss Brown, he started it. Anyway, he ain't hurt."

"Just sit down and be quiet. That's all I ask of you," said our Miss Brown wearily. Once we quieted down, she was content to talk to the front-row girls and over-look our absorption in *Sport* magazine or Mark Harris's baseball novels, *The Southpaw* and *Bang the Drum Slowly,* two hardbacks we "borrowed" from the library and read at least a half dozen times. We devoured the *Sporting News,* the old-timey bible of baseball facts and figures, and took an open-minded view of the upstart *Sports Illustrated,* born in 1955. But our heart's darling was still the venerable *Sport* magazine.

Such books and magazines were allowed in class, but Miss Brown drew the line at anyone reading a "dirty" book, which to her mind was virtually any paperback with a lurid cover, books like *God's Little Acre* or *Tobacco Road* or anything by that "filthy-minded man" Mickey Spillane. Anybody caught reading that trash in her class would be sent to the principal's office on the spot. She needn't have worried. Erskine Caldwell was a pop-up compared to Mark Harris.

One day I stumbled across a worn, dog-eared paperback dictionary in the hall. I picked it up and asked Gino and Ralphie Joe and several of my other buddies if they knew anyone who'd lost such a book. They said no, they didn't even know anybody who had one. I had no use for it, but I pitched it in my locker.

Several days later I was sitting in Miss Brown's study hall, a large section held in the school auditorium. It was the middle of the day. Nothing much had happened. Boredom, no stranger to anyone in study hall except the college bound, began to creep around the auditorium. Then a brilliant, beautiful idea came to me.

I arose from my seat, walked down to Miss Brown's desk, and asked her permission to go to the bathroom. She wasn't pleased with my request but said, "Don't be all day. Get back here and do some studying."

Yes, Miss Brown.

I dashed to my locker. I fished out that dictionary. I scrunched it under my arm so that old eagle-eye Brown with her extra-thick glasses that magnified her big round eyes would just barely be able to see it. As I sauntered by her desk, I cast a sheepish eye her way. When I reached my seat I slumped as far down as I could, opened my magazine, put my dictionary behind it, and pretended to

read—and waited. It didn't take long.

"You, young man," she said, pointing an angry, snapping finger in my direction. "What book did you bring in here just now? What are you reading?"

"I'm just studying my book, Miss Brown," I said, looking up at her but keeping my dictionary out of sight. The room went silent.

"You come down here this moment," she fired back, "and bring that dirty book with you."

"Now, Miss Brown," I replied haltingly, "this isn't what you think. It's a book I need for English class." She knew good and well I was lying. When had I ever read anything for any English class? She was halfway convinced and partly right that English was a foreign language to me.

"You bring that book down here right now," she fired back, her voice rising. "Don't think you can pull the wool over my eyes. Come down here this instant!"

I arose slowly and ambled down the aisle, already savoring my coming triumph. I held the book behind me. When I arrived at her desk I hesitantly handed it to her, saying it was just something important I needed for a term paper.

She snatched the book from my hand, glanced at it, then looked at it solemnly. Fury reddened her face. Slowly she raised her eyes to meet mine. She stared at me for a long moment—those big eyes snapping—and then barked, "Get back to your seat."

Miss Brown was down, but was she down for the count? When I moseyed into her history class the next day she looked at me as if I were a communist or something. She said not a word, she just stared at me. I went to the back of the room, sat down, and opened a magazine and

began reading. Class went on as usual: she talked to the girls on the front row and several college-bound boys who sat near the front. She uttered not a word to me or my buddies in the amen section. Several weeks went by and all remained quiet on the western front.

Then it was time for our six-week grade report and I braced for the tongue-lashing the old man would dish out when he saw my string of M's. At the end of the hour Miss Brown said she had our cards marked and ready for us to take on to our next class. But, she announced in a voice of ice water, she would like to see me for just a moment.

When I came to her desk she gave me the evil eye and held out my card but refused to let go of it. "I don't like the subpar level of your work," she said, prompting me to wonder what "work" she had in mind. "And I don't like your attitude." She was giving me a grade of I, she went on, and if I didn't shape up, would make that Inferior an F the next time, which just happened to be the grade report for the semester.

"Aren't you on the basketball team?" she asked, still clutching my grade card.

"Yes, ma'am," I told her. Something told me it was time to be extra polite.

Well, she knew that, though she didn't go to the games. She had more important things to do. But she'd talked to Coach Huhn, the same man who had flailed me with the towel several weeks back. He shared her view that I needed waking up, even failed, if she thought best. Thanks, Coach!

"So take this grade as a warning. Because should you get an F for this semester you'll be ineligible; you won't be playing any sports next term, and probably won't

graduate, either, will you? You'll have to go to summer school." With that she plunged a dagger in my heart, and she knew it.

Don't go crying to Coach Huhn, I told myself. "Chalky" (given to chewing nervously on a piece of chalk during a tense game) was always going on about how he had no time for stupid ballplayers and how it was our responsibility to stay eligible to play. He wouldn't lift a finger to change Miss Brown's mind. He'd probably make me run extra laps after practice "so you can think about what your teacher told you."

I mumbled something to Miss Brown about doing better during the upcoming six weeks and walked away in a daze. Not be eligible? That was a fate worse than death, Gino and my teammates agreed. Just who does she think she is? She can't get away with that! Can she? Yup.

I hotfooted it to Miss Brown to ask what I needed to do to make amends, to get an M for the semester. She knew exactly what I needed to do. In addition to reading the textbook—oh, horror!—and coming to class pre-pared to say something, I was to copy out entries on American history from a fat encyclopedia in the school library. And I was to pick meaty pieces that pertained to what we were doing in class. "And not just a bunch of short entries, either," she snapped. I was to hand in three a week until she was satisfied with my attitude. Also, I was to sit on the front row. God Almighty, she knew how to get her pound of flesh. She was tougher than the old man at grade-card time, meaner than Old Man Pierce. I cursed that damned dictionary.

But I was sure the joke was on her. She excused me from study hall and told me to go to the library and start reading and copying the encyclopedia. I was pretty sure

I could goof off in the stacks with someone. But it turned out that Miss Brown had tipped off the librarian. I had to sit at a table near her desk.

But then something strange happened. After a while, I didn't mind thumbing through the encyclopedia, reading and copying out my weekly quota. Some entries bordered on being, well, almost interesting. Andrew Jackson, "Old Hickory," wasn't too bad; he was no Neat Guy. Neither was this lunatic John Brown. The old boy was crazy as a bedbug, but when they hanged him he didn't cry like a baby. Abraham Lincoln made for good reading, too, but I wasn't up to copying out his entire life. There was all that Civil War business.

But I was cool. I didn't utter a peep to any of my pals—some of whom volunteered to sit with me in the library—that some tiny part of me had come to enjoy, even look forward to, my daily sessions with the encyclopedia.

Then, midway through my incarceration in the library, heaven began to smile on me. One of the prettiest college-bound girls started coming in every day. Soon she began choosing a chair across the table from me. What's happening here? For most of the year, I had drooled just thinking about her. But she knew I was a clown. She was not only a knockout, she was a class officer, a wheel in the elite Literary Society—someone, said her admirers, so brainy she could "write her own ticket to any college." The book on her was that she had a lock on being valedictorian. So what's she doing sitting close to me?

I glanced up from my absorption in the encyclopedia and smiled at her. She smiled back. What was I doing, she wondered. Oh, studying. I tried to sound noncha-

lant. Did I come here every day at this time? Oh yes, I replied, I'm doing some special work for history. "It's my favorite class." (Don't push it, you big dummy!)

She liked history too, but English was her favorite. She liked to write poetry. Gee, me too. Well, I mean, I like reading it now and then. And I love English, too. I really like *Ivanhoe*. Did she? He's great, isn't he? Who, she said, Ivanhoe or Sir Walter Scott? Oh, both, both are really good. Who's my favorite character in the book, other than Ivanhoe? Well, now, that's a tough one to answer, there are so many great ones.

Was all this happening to me? Could this cute, pretty, popular, beautiful, sexy—she radiated loveliness in those cashmere sweaters—brainy, college-bound, valedictorian-in-the-making actually be sitting here whispering to me? Did it mean anything? She was probably taking pity on me. She was known to be really polite, even to idiots and morons. She probably knew that Miss Brown had banished me to the library.

I didn't know. But the next day I made sure to wear my letter sweater—the white one with the big purple N on the front—on the off chance I might shine some in her eyes. On the fourth or fifth day I screwed up my courage and asked her if she was doing anything that weekend and would she like to go see a movie and have a Coke and hamburger. She said yes. Thank you, thank you, thank you, God!

"What does she see in you, you big ape?" Ralphie Joe demanded to know.

"I don't know, but we're going on a date, a real date," I answered proudly.

It was the letter sweater that won her over. Or perhaps it was my reputation for being a class clown—they say

It was the letter sweater that won her over.

brainy, nice girls have a soft spot in their hearts for cutups. Perhaps her religious upbringing—her older brother was bound for the Baptist pulpit—propelled her to think she could reform me.

I didn't care what the reason was. I was in love. On the spot. In love. Years later she told it was my burr haircut. I didn't believe her. Still don't. (Whatever it was, we were married a few years later.)

At the end of the semester, just about the time writer's cramp was beginning to set in, Miss Brown said that she was satisfied with my work. No more bouts with the encyclopedia, "unless, of course, you want to." Well, now, I'll have to think about that. But she said sternly

that she was refusing to give me an M. No, I had changed so much that she was elevating me to the rarefied air of the college bound by marking a solid S on my grade card. How about that! But not even she could bring herself to reward me with the highest mark, E for Excellent.

"Do you know why I made you do all that extra work?" she asked me at the beginning of the new semester.

"Because of that dirty, rotten trick I played on you with the dictionary," I answered.

"Only partly," she said, her face giving in to a hint of a smile. "I know you never do any schoolwork, and all you think about is sports and girls, but I think you have some potential. You might even have a brain." Had I ever thought about that?

No, I told her, not quite truthfully.

"Well, think about it," Miss Brown said. "You know, you don't have to be like all your buddies if you don't want to."

I shrugged and thanked her, walked out the door, and made my way to my next class, thinking some, but not much, about what she had said. Potential. Now there's the sort of worrisome word the old man could get going on.

Potential? I had it—in baseball. I was pretty sure of that. But I was also uneasily aware that for some unfathomable reason I felt odd, different from my friends, not smarter (for God's sake) or better, just different. Inside, where it didn't show. In some weird way I felt slightly out of step with everyone else. Everyone. Even Gino and Ralphie Joe and everyone in the Riding Around Gang. Maybe it was because of the old man's strange ways, or Mom's combination of generosity and hard-line rules, or growing up in the Church of Christ, or being more of a maniac about baseball than all of my friends put together, even those who were clearly better players than I was.

My sunny side told me that everyone in school felt unique. My darker side caused me to think that just about everybody else in school, or at least among the kids I hung out with, was hopelessly simple and headed for barber college or the Ford plant. Like father, like son, I guess.

So I put it out of my mind. I didn't think much at all about the sort of thing Miss Brown called potential. That could be shoved easily into sometime in the hazy future. I was, after all, a cutup, a clown with a reputation to maintain.

Still, there was something in Miss Brown's words that rumbled around in the back of what passed for my mind. And at the end of the year, when our school yearbooks came out and everybody dashed around madly getting their pals' autographs and words of undying friendship—"always stay the great guy you are!"—I committed an unpardonable sin. I didn't even tell any of the Riding Around Gang, but on the sly I asked Miss Brown if she would be willing to sign my yearbook. She looked surprised, pondered my request for a moment—she may have thought I was putting her on—and then wrote beside her picture: "You will make it, I think. Good luck to a fine fellow." I thanked her and never told a soul what I had done.

That was several months later. For the moment I had more important things to do than to trouble my mind with potential. There was "Greasy" Graves to be made as miserable as possible. Mr. Graves—with his fondness for oily, greasy kid stuff to manage his thick, curly hair—was earnestness all over. Although young, he had obviously gone off his rocker. He had the insane idea that all of his students would learn world history.

This was intolerable. Why hadn't Greasy learned from our other teachers? In English class we were assigned successive chapters of *Ivanhoe* throughout the semester. But never once, not once, did we discuss one word of the book. Each day in class our teacher said he had something important to work on and would we read quietly for the hour. He also had a small closet in the back of the room. He would disappear in there once or twice a class session. What's he doing in there, I muttered, thinking of Mr. Jim, "taking a shit, shave, and a shampoo?"

Greasy Graves announced that we would read the chapters of our history books "as homework" and have spirited discussions. No can do. We took an oath: say nothing in class. Anyway, the girls in the front row would talk enough. When he resorted to yelling at those of us in the back rows, demanding that we say something intelligent, we decided it was time to declare war.

One day a week we were to read in class and then discuss *Junior Scholastic,* or some such weekly newspaper with news of the big world in it. While we read, Greasy worked on his grade book or lesson plan or whatever he did to ready himself to teach even the imbeciles in the back rows. But we had a surprise attack.

As soon as he put his nose in his notes we held our newspapers out in front of us as loosely as possible. Then when one of our number nodded, we opened them as hard as we could. Snap! By the time Greasy's head jerked up in shock we would all be holding our papers in front of our faces, our eyes glued to the page. "There's lots of good things in this weekly reader; did you know that

Mr. Graves?" one of us would pipe up right after he shouted, "Who did that?" The rest of us had our heads buried in the paper, too absorbed in all that wonderful news of the world even to notice Greasy Graves's words.

"I'm warning you boys, I don't like that. It's highly disrespectful, rude, not only to me but to your classmates who actually *want* an education."

He returned to his grade book, shaking his head at the hooligans he had to teach. But in the earliest days of our prank he was sure he could win us over.

"Snap!" His head jerked up the next time we did it. But he looked casually at his watch and returned to his work, hoping to shame us out of silliness by ignoring us.

"Snap!" "Snap!" "Snap!" we fired back.

Now he could take it no longer. He jumped up from his chair and bolted for the door, yelling that he was headed for the principal's office. We were going to be sorry.

He returned with one of the vice principals in tow, a former coach who knew most of us well, and liked many of us. "Now what's going on here, boys," the beefy ex-coach asked cheerfully. "Mr. Graves says you are turning the pages of your *Junior Scholastic* rudely, and disturbing the rest of the class."

Nobody had any idea what Mr. Graves was talking about. We liked our newspaper. Why, Mr. Graves, hadn't we just told you that there was lots of good stuff in this paper?

After that Greasy Graves gave up and talked to the four or five girls in the front row. The war was over. From then on, when he handed out our newspapers we read *The Southpaw* or *Sport* magazine. Oh, once in a while, when Greasy was lost in his papers or, better yet, nodding off for a short nap, we looked at each other and "Snap!"

Greasy Graves shouldn't have taken our shenanigans personally. We liked him. We had tortures devised for all of our teachers—all of them, that is, except the coaches who taught remedial math, or something called "human science." Those guys, most of them big fellows, felt no compunction whatsoever about grabbing an offender and shoving him against the lockers just as soon as they found him in the gym.

In typing class, where everyone was timed in the ever-lasting hope that we would get to sixty words a minute—fat chance!—we devised strategies to divert the teacher's attention. Then we swiped her alarm clock and passed it around the room, placing it under some Neat Guy's chair just seconds before the alarm was to sound. When she prevented that trick by clutching the alarm clock, we passed the room's various reference books to the guys sitting in the row by the windows. In spring and fall, when the furnaces were working overtime, we flipped the books out the open windows. One day a pigeon flew in and flew neurotically around the room as we yelled and screamed, "Get out, get out, this is a typing class!"

We made life really miserable for Miss Pickens. Poor Miss Pickens was short and dumpy and, to our cool view of the world, so far out of it, she'd never get back in. From day one, we dubbed her Miss Slim Pickens and adroitly slurred the words into one. "Hey, MsSlimPickens, I've gotta go to the bathroom. Now!"

She was a substitute math teacher who had the misfortune to inherit Coach Henry's remedial math class when he was promoted to vice principal midway through the semester. But when stocky MsSlimPickens walked into class there were a couple of things she didn't know: first, Coach Henry, a huge man, was a great guy who had mastered a relaxed attitude toward teaching. He enjoyed spending the hour talking about either the last game the Northeast Vikings had played or the upcoming one. And, second, most of us in the class had passed the school system's mandated Junior Math Test—you had to be extra stupid not to pass that—and had signed up for remedial math just to have a do-nothing class.

When Miss Pickens marched in the door that first day we spied a worthy rival. She announced that all of us would learn. To see to it, we'd have daily exams. Okay. War. We love it. Here's our battle plan: everyone turn in blank papers to her. Every day we had a test; every day we turned the sheets back in to her totally blank. She stormed. She ranted. "Your tests are too hard," we told her. "This is remedial math, remember!"

After several days of pitched battle she threatened to go to Mr. Henry and rat on us. We told her that was probably not going to work. Coach Henry, "Old Reliable" in our view, didn't let us down. He came to class and rambled on some about the upcoming game and were we ready? We are, Coach. Sorry, MsSlimPickens. But we tried to tell you.

Sadly, my pals and I were not involved in the most notorious, glorious act of idiocy that occurred during my misspent days at Northeast High School. Another group of no-goods decided that the imposing, larger-than-life hall statues of George Washington and Abraham Lincoln needed a little something. To that end they employed their woodworking skills with the lathe and chisel. Then they slipped into the school at night and suitably adorned the Father of Our Country and the Great Emancipator.

The next morning every idiot and moron at Northeast

High School was tickled pink. There stood Washington and Lincoln, great men we were to emulate in every way, sporting giant erections. I mean, we're talking big, wow! "No wonder Big George is called the father of our country."

Of course the top-dog administrators, even Coach Henry, huffed and puffed and ordered the maintenance men to do their duty. Our principals assured the assembled student body that the nasty perpetrators—whom everybody assumed to be some of our own students—would be found out and punished. But who were they? Would they be real men—true Vikings—and come forth and acknowledge their dirty deed? (No, of course not!) Did anybody know who did it and would they tell? (No, of course not. Are you crazy or something!) No one was going to be a rat fink. Everyone stood in awe of the pranksters and wished they'd thought of the joke themselves.

Our student government leaders sniffed their disapproval of this moral desecration—though they, like everybody else, probably had a pretty good idea of who had done it. But they weren't saying. And so the great mystery remained unsolved.

Many years later, some other group broke into the school in the middle of the night with real meanness on their minds. They lugged in sledgehammers or baseball bats and smashed most of the trophy cases. They also turned their ugly anger on George Washington and Abraham Lincoln and bashed them to pieces. Those majestic statues have never been replaced.

17

Indian Ball and Poker Days

What moments of our youth would we live over again? What if, when we returned to those golden moments, we could feel exactly as we did then? Nothing would have changed; nor could we change anything. We would not be allowed to say I'm sorry or take back any hurtful words. Nor would we know the future, any part of it. We would be as we were then—we wouldn't have an old body, a complaining tongue, graying hair, or a personality fixed and inflexible. Our minds would be innocent of irony or paradox but not of our youthful illusions. What moment would it be?

I'm not sure. Would it be to stand silently, breathlessly, in the dark and peep at Big Red? Or sit and talk baseball with Mr. Jim, or jam with the Bowery Boys, or loll on the front porch swing with my grandmother and eat an orange? What about reliving that first moment of love—the first rush of being in love, the first embraces, the first kisses, that first feel of forbidden roundness. I think about it.

I confess: I would love to hit baseballs again. I'd like to

wake up and discover it's spring, say, of 1955 or 1956. The house is quiet. The folks have left for work. The sun is shining, the clouds have gone; it's going to be a warm day. I am in heaven.

The telephone rings and, yes, it's true, the voice on the other end is Gino's. He's already talked to Ralphie Joe, who agrees: today is too fine a day to waste on school. I'll call Shortcake and tell him our plans. It will be done—exactly as it was then.

A warm sunny day in April or May is a perfect day to "ditch" school and have a game of "Indian ball" and later get in a serious session of penny-ante poker. This is living!

I make my telephone calls. All we need for a good game of Indian ball is four, but five or six is okay.

No need to hurry. The outfield grass will be wet with dew until midmorning. That gives us just enough time to drive—I'm back in my '49 Chevy—or take the bus downtown to Elliott's Sporting Goods Store to look over the new cleats and gloves, the new jerseys, jackets, and baseball caps. We don't need a cap. We now sport our team's new hats, but it's fun trying them on and preening before the mirror. Grabbing a new Louisville Slugger or this year's new model Adirondack bats, we use the mirrors to study our batting stances and offer helpful suggestions to each other.

But we have more serious things to do than kill time as we check out the new hats. We examine each new bat, checking its weight and length. How's the grain look? Who's name is on it—is it a Stan Musial model or a Mickey Mantle? That doesn't matter. It's got to feel just right in the hands. What's it cost?

"Sir, could you come over here and give us some

help?" The salesman walks over, eager to make a sale, apparently indifferent to his own question: shouldn't you boys be in school? The trick is to ask him several questions at once. Do you have this thirty-four-ounce beauty in a thirty-three? How come this Louisville Slugger costs more than that Adirondack over there? Didn't you used to carry this lightweight one in a Ted Kluszewski model? You didn't? I'm sure I saw one down here the last time we were in. It was a week ago. Maybe it was two weeks. Come on, you remember. We bought a big son of a gun, a big Kluszewski number that time.

The plan is for two or three of us to rattle off questions machine-gun style and get the poor man worrying about bats, lots of bats, big ones and medium-size ones. "Remember, we don't want any size under a thirty-three, okay?" He seems the sort to remember that much.

"You don't know whether you have this one, this thirty-four, in a thirty-three in the storage room?" No? "Well, why not go and ask that guy over there at the cash register to go look for you."

"Hey, I hate to bother you, but do you have a Roy Campanella catcher's mitt? What about a Del Crandall model? All I see over here is a Yogi Berra. No Campanella? Man, that's hard to believe!"

"Is this the only size this hat comes in? Where do you keep your warm-up jackets? I don't see any extra larges, just a bunch of mediums and larges."

Is the poor guy rattled yet? That's the goal. Get the salesman nervous, get him nervous in the service. Get him so he doesn't know whether he's coming or going as he tries to decide which question to answer first while trying to figure out whether to go ask the other clerk about their inventory or to hustle to the back room to look for that thirty-three-ounce bat himself. When he's really flustered—that's the time to strike.

"Hey, here it is, over here," one of us yells out, holding up a sleek new bat. "Somebody misshelved this thirty-three Louisville Slugger." Now everybody in the store is looking toward the bat section and wondering how'd that bat get over there. "Here's the bat we've been looking for. I'll take it. Who do I pay? You or the other guy?"

With clerks turning instinctively toward the bat section or the cash register to ring up the sale, one of us slips a brand-new baseball into our jacket pocket and starts to amble for the door. Don't rush, don't run. Don't worry, we've done this before. We're pros—at least at swiping a brand-new baseball. We've never been caught. We don't intend to start now.

Riding toward Lykins Park we turn the new baseball over and over again in our hands, admiring our treasure. How comfortable a brand-new gleaming white baseball feels in the hand. We don't fool around; we always make sure to swipe good stuff, official American League baseballs. We can hit this baby all morning, hit it a mile.

Don't we have any remorse, feel just a little bit guilty? No. Didn't then. Felt good.

Indian ball is wonderfully simple to play. It needs just two to a side, with one group playing the field—with an infielder and an outfielder—while the other bats. Your teammate pitches to you and tries to serve up down-the-middle fast balls you can clobber. Each batter gets three outs; then you pitch to your partner until he makes three outs. Any swing and a miss is an out. So is any ground ball cleanly fielded on the infield, any fly ball caught, or anything hit to the right of an imaginary line from home plate through second base to dead-center field.

I suppose you could strike out, but we didn't. The pitcher was your teammate, remember, grooving medium-speed pitches to you. We hit sharp ground balls past the infielder. Or line drives that bounced in front of the outfielder. Those were singles. Four of 'em and you had a run. Any ball hit over the outfielder's head was a home run.

We played with a half dozen or so balls, some of them scuffed and even soft, some covered with black electrical tape. These taped balls were too heavy to hit for any distance. You didn't have to tell your pitcher to throw you the old balls first—you could usually sneak in a couple of singles hitting those dead balls, particularly if you could handle the bat well enough to hit sharp line drives.

Three singles. Bases loaded. Now, Gino, throw me that new sweetheart. Is there any greater joy on earth than really smacking a brand-new, still-white, official American League baseball? Those babies fly. I mean, you know the moment you feel the bat hit the ball when you've really tagged one. It feels good all over. Hit it hard. It's gone.

In Indian ball you don't have to run to first. Or run anywhere. You just stand there after you've hit a towering fly ball to left field and yell, "Get out! Get out! Get out of here!" Often it does. That brand-new official American League baseball zooms over Shorty's or Ralphie Joe's head for a grand slam. Four runs in on one swing of the bat. As that baby soars all they can do is watch it and weep—and wait for their turn at bat when they get to hit that new ball.

Indian ball is perfect baseball. You hit. Forced to hit those lumpy or taped balls? Then choke up on the bat and hit ground balls down the third-base line and just beyond the reach of the infielder. Is he wise to you? Is he cheating over toward the third-base line? Quick, adjust your stance and drive one near the middle. Be careful. Don't hit one to the right of second base or you make an out.

I repeat, Indian ball is perfect baseball. You field. As the only infielder you often get to dive in the dust for skidding ground balls. You can pull off some astounding plays. Ignore that dust in your mouth. Roaming the outfield, positioning is everything. What ball is going to be pitched? An old one? Run in, play shallow. Go on, just try to hit that beanbag over my head for a homer. Watch it. The pitcher just reached down for that new baseball. Get back. Get back. Play as deep as you can.

Playing a deep left field at Lykins was a great part of the fun. The park was bounded by city streets; the yard across the street from left field inclined sharply—just like at old Crosley Field in Cincinnati, we told ourselves. The greatest catches were those you pulled off by running across the street—you just hoped no cars were coming— and catching the ball as you scrambled up the hill. Many a grand slam has been stabbed in the heart by one of those Willie Mays catches by a young Yankee hopeful.

The game lasts until we're ready to drop—drop everything and eat, that is. A quick stop at Chernikoff's Grocery Store and we're set for lunch. We have two or three loaves of Italian bread, each to be sliced in half and piled high with bologna, salami, cheese, potato chips, pickles, lettuce, mustard, mayonnaise, ketchup, or anything we can scavenge from the icebox of the house we know is safest—usually Ralphie Joe's. Most of the grownups on his block work all day and won't be around to report us to our parents or the school principal.

The feast over, it's time for some serious poker playing. There's still a couple of hours before school is out. We've got a couple of decks of cards, a couple of rolls of pennies each, and a feeling that this just might be the day we win and win big. We play deuces wild or one-eyed jacks wild—sometimes in the same hand. The dealer gets to announce the game and the rules. Five-card stud. Only two cards from the dealer. Black nines wild. Seven-card stud. Low card in the hole wild, of course, but, let's see, red threes wild, too.

Come on, ante up. Two cents each. Cards coming. Who'll open? You will? Good. Let's see some money, then. Three cents. Three cents? Man, I see your puny three-cent bet and raise you two more dirty coppers. You in, Ralphie Joe? Gino, you want a card? You got to put a nickel out there, Kemo Sabe. Come on, Tonto, get in the game pronto. You gotta stop drinking that Kickapoo Joy Juice if you want to have a clear head for poker. I'm in, I'm in! You got nothing. Cards coming.

Two for you, Gino, three for you, Ralphie Joe. You opened and you want, how many, four cards! You gotta be kiddin' me. The man who raised the bet wants one. One card? What are you holding over there? Dealer takes one. You heard me, I'm takin' one. Got dandruff! Some of it itches! Stop saying that! I told you, 'tain't funny, McGee.

You opened. You betting or just sittin' there pissin' in your pants? I opened but he raised me. He bets first. The man here, with a hand you won't believe until you see it, bets five cents. That's right. One whole Indian head nickel, my friend. You're bluffin'. You got nothin'. You want to see my nothin'? It's goin' to cost you five big ones, five centavos, amigo. I'm out. Me too. Too rich for me. Hey, you thought I was bluffin'! Changed my mind. Hand's over. You win.

You mean you guys ain't even curious to see what I'm holding? No, jughead, we ain't payin' to see your hand. You gave it away, you big dummy, when you raised the bet and took only one card. Hell, only a numskull wouldn't know you're holding two pairs. But what if I had four spades and drew a club or a red card? What about that? There ain't nothin' about that. Because I doubt very much that you had anything but two pairs. Your thinking you could sucker us in was nothing but a fig newton of your imagination. I'm telling you you gave your hand away when you raised the first bet. Poker's about finesse, my friend. Time for another hand. When are you ever going to learn? Learn? Man, I learned a lot today, didn't I? I didn't go to school.

Does this golden day have to end? It does, but not quite yet. There's baseball practice after dinner. What about a session with the pinball machines at Frank's Filthy Restaurant? Anyone for shooting baskets by the streetlight later tonight?

We'll go to bed and drift off to sleep listening to Larry Ray announce the A's game over the radio. We'll dream about hitting baseballs for the Yankees someday. Now, that will be the best day of all. Sorry. We just had the best day of all. But we won't know that until we wake up many, many years later.

18

"Run 'Em Out, Boy, Always Run 'Em Out"

The end came suddenly. Abruptly. Cruelly. I should have seen it coming, grasped the hard, unyielding truth, but it was too awful, and I had turned my eyes away from a brute fact that everybody else around me probably saw clearly.

I thought I had seen fast balls. I had. At the birth of my passionate embrace of baseball, had I not stood but a few feet away and watched legends of the mound, the very best the Blues and the A's had? I had seen and I had heard: heard blazing fast balls smack into catchers' mitts. How I loved that sound. Wide-eyed I had seen Warren Spahn, Herb Score, Mike Garcia, Arnie Portocarrero, Ewell "the Whip" Blackwell, Bob Feller, and Bobby Shantz pitch. These immortals, large and small, were what I would become—such had been my dreamy state of desire, my intense and exquisite longing to be a ballplayer. Someday. It had to be.

At fifteen and sixteen I had caught some guys who could throw hard, so hard I put a special pad inside the palm of my catcher's mitt. Even so my hand was often

"Prospects" were to show
up in uniform.

red and swollen after a game. I had caught Jack Kirby, a righty, and Larry Dierking, a lefty, sandlot legends in Northeast. I had caught and batted against John O'Donahue, a big southpaw who would one day stand on the mound for the Royals, Kansas City's team after 1968. So, by the summer of 1956, fast balls, curve balls, knuckle balls held no terrors for me.

That summer the St. Louis Cardinals conducted a camp in Municipal Stadium. It was an open tryout— come one, come all. Come you young dreamers and show your stuff. "Prospects" were to show up in uniform and cap and bring a glove and spikes. A "pro scout" would be on hand to evaluate the hopefuls. It would be my big day. I would show the world, prove the old man wrong, and hasten my ascent toward heaven.

On my big day, my Chevy was in the shop so I took the bus. I went alone. I couldn't persuade any of my buddies to come along. I got off the bus at Fifteenth and Brooklyn and walked the seven blocks to the big stadium, through the black section of Kansas City, a trek I had made many times before to see the Blues or the A's play. I took no thought of the neighborhood or of the obscenity I was: a big white boy with a flattop wearing a uniform from the city league that barred black kids from its ranks. I walked on. I was in a dream—technicolor for me. Black and white for everyone else.

The hopefuls entered the ballpark through the wide gate in center field, the same gate the great and the near great had strolled through. I crossed the warning track and stood on the outfield grass: where the Mick had stood; and Ted Williams and Big Gus Zernial. Here mighty men, mighty gods had trod. And now I was walking there, too, on my way to showing the

Cardinals what I was made of.

The old scout directing the camp was no boy of summer, no Apollo, not now. Where once had been sleekness and rippling muscles were now jowls and fat. A mountainous belly bulged dangerously over his belt. He hitched up his pants, again and again, a battle he would have to fight all day long. But he was a "pro scout." The man to please.

When he took off his snazzy red Cardinals baseball cap to rub his sweaty forehead he revealed a dismayingly bald head, the skin alarmingly mottled from too many days in the sun. Tobacco protruded from his jaw. That wad shifted from side to side, usually right before he spit. A brownish stain marked his lip and chin. Still, he was the man to please.

He yelled out orders in a brisk manner, barking instructions, organizing the tryout, a clipboard in one hand, a stubby pencil in the other. He didn't smile. At his side stood another uniformed old-timer and two young, sleek, bronzed ballplayers in Cardinals uniforms. Sign-up sheets came first. Height. Weight. Age. Position. Left-handed or right. "Fill 'em out, fellows, and hand 'em back in."

Pitchers and catchers, over here by home plate. Outfielders, out there. Infielders, let's put you guys out by second base. I took my place by home plate. I was a catcher who still dreamed of being a pitcher. But this was no time to bring that up.

I recognized a few faces, guys I had played against, a couple of pitchers I had faced. As a catcher, I could handle these guys. As a batter, I could hit these guys. This day had been a long time coming, and I intended to make the most of it.

Most of the other hopefuls were strangers to me, tall and short guys in unfamiliar uniforms—some shabby, faded, and baggy with the names of hardware stores or funeral homes on the front or back. Where had these clodhoppers come from? From nearby Missouri towns, that's where—from Peculiar, Bogart, Lexington, Napoleon; from St. Joe, Liberty, Raytown; from Waverly; from Moberly, I overheard one say. Another mentioned that he had come up from Joplin and that this was his fifth tryout camp. "How many have you been to?" he asked. None, I said, and sounded stupid.

Some looked like ballplayers. But some were beefy fat, some were too short, some looked suspiciously like they had been shaving for a few years. Several were country boys—those oversize flat-as-a-pancake ball gloves gave them away. I hadn't seen mitts like those since the last time I watched *The Babe Ruth Story* or *Pride of the Yankees*. Some of the gloves had new rawhide stringing. Several Cardinal wannabes had no cleats.

How can you play baseball, try out for the St. Louis Cardinals, in those big black high-top tennis shoes? Not everyone wore the proper socks and stirrups; their hairy legs were bare between their tennis shoes and pants. Who are these guys trying to fool? I was prepared, properly attired. Clean uniform. Nice hat. Real cleats. Well-oiled catcher's mitt. This was my day.

"Catchers and pitchers, start warming up. We're going to divide all you guys up into two teams and have a little ball game." The old scout and his assistant called out the names. We were to take the field when we heard our names called out. Until then, sit in the dugout. "Before the day's over, everybody will get a chance to play an inning in the field and bat at least once."

All those who thought they were pitchers were to trot down with a couple of catchers to the bull pen, where the assistant scout would look them over as they threw. "He'll tell me how you look, tell me if you got potential," said the fat man who held the destiny of each of us in those chubby hands and fingers.

Then we were told that we were not going to hit against one of our own. No, the old scout had another idea: we would all take our cuts against a couple of youngsters the Cardinals had recently signed, "these boys right here," said the old man, pointing to the young men in Cardinals uniforms. So that's who they were. Rookie phenoms. Pro ball players. Even better, I thought.

One of the pitchers was a big right-hander, the other a slender, pint-size lefty cut from the mold of Bobby Shantz. As they warmed up on the sidelines their every pitch snapped in the catchers' gloves.

Suddenly, out of the blue, that snap began to sound ominous. Moisture started dripping off the tip of my nose. Sweat ran down the back of my neck. My armpits felt hot and clammy. Without warning, I felt an urge to start walking (no, running) as fast as I could toward center field and the gate that just minutes before had seemed so welcoming. What on earth had made me think I could compete with these guys and impress a real scout? Who was I kidding? Who had I been kidding for years? My fingers tingled. My hat felt too tight. My head felt hot. My hair was on fire.

I glanced over my shoulder at the lefty as he finished warming up. He had a streaking fast ball, a vicious downward breaking curve. The big right-hander seemed to be concentrating on his fast ball. Then, mysteriously, I felt okay. Maybe I could hit these guys, these rookies. They weren't much older than I was. A surge of optimism, of confidence, came over me. Of the two, I thought I preferred batting against the right-hander.

I wasn't in the first batch to play in the field or get a chance at the plate. Just as well. The first pitcher was the southpaw. He struck out most of the batters he faced. Both righties and lefties had trouble making contact with his pitches, and several left-handed hitters lurched out of the batter's box when he threw his knifing curve. One by one they trudged back to the dugout shaking their heads in sorrow. In disbelief.

I told myself: if you have to hit against this guy go up looking for his fast ball and swing hard. But, judging by the number of players who were called to bat, I began to think I wouldn't have to hit against him and his wicked curve ball.

By the time my name was called the little lefty had departed and the right-hander, who looked even bigger standing out there on the mound, was pitching. But still I felt good. I was ready. I liked the bat I had picked out. When my name was barked out I hustled to the plate. Watch out world. I can hit this guy.

Before stepping into the batter's box I looked down at the old, pudgy scout who was coaching the game, clipboard in hand, from the first-base coaching box. "Let's see what you can do, big boy." I nodded and stepped in to take my cuts, to show my stuff.

I dug in at the plate. The lanky right-hander on the mound took his signal, wound up, kicked his left leg high, and let fly. Pop! I recognized that sound. That was the snap of a fast ball crashing into the catcher's mitt. But all I knew was that something ridiculously small and round had zipped over the plate. Was it really a baseball?

Something the size of an aspirin had smacked into the catcher's mitt. Whatever it was, it exploded in my ear.

"Strike one," the umpire bellowed in a voice that surely heaven could hear. I was in shock. Total terror. I had never seen or heard any fast ball like that one. My hands, once dry and confident, were drenched. The bat had become slippery. I stepped out of the box and tried to regain some composure. I tried mightily not to let anyone see that I was shaking as I bent over to pick up dirt and rub it into my hands. Now, I could at least grip the bat. Stepping back into the batter's box, I kicked the dirt and dug in my back foot with great determination born of terror and a creeping feeling of doom.

The pitcher went into his windup, kicked his leg toward the sky, and whistled what I think was a sharp breaking ball. It must have nicked the outside corner of the plate. I heard that fateful snap again and the umpire's yell, "Strike two." The man seemed to be enjoying his job as he bellowed out his calls in a voice that seemed to reverberate around the stadium and up into the highest reaches of where I'd sat through many a Blues game and to the spot where I had seen Larry Doby break Ewell Blackwell's heart the year before.

Fear, anxiety, terror, dread. Each exploded in my heart and tore me apart. My eyes burned. No amount of dust dried my palms. I could hardly lift the bat. My feet felt cramped. I was down to my last strike. I dug in for my last confrontation with Zeus on the mound. Bravely but numbly, I awaited his last thunderbolt. All calm, all confidence, all hope had now vanished. One more pitch and I would be gone. Gone forever.

I prayed. I squinted. I blinked my eyes to wash away the salty sweat. I needed every ounce of luck and sight I could squeeze from this last confrontation with destiny. The kid on the mound looked like a giant now. He nodded to the catcher, wound up, and let fly. The aspirin hurtled toward the plate.

I swung. I heard and felt the bat hit the ball. To my utter astonishment I had hit it. But it was an anemic pop fly to center field. It wasn't a real hit. The sound of the bat hitting the ball told me that. In that one-millionth of a second I knew I had failed, failed completely, miserably. My hands, my arms, my body knew it before my brain.

I remained frozen at the plate. I stood woodenly and watched the arc of that puny fly ball drifting lazily toward center field. Despair gripped me and wouldn't let go. All of my instincts, my knowledge of baseball, my untold hours of hitting baseballs said run, run to first base. But a despair far deeper than knowledge or even instinct had me in a vise. I stood there motionless as though someone had knocked me senseless. Someone had. I was senseless.

Then instinct took over. But only barely. The bat fell from my hands and I headed for first base. But I didn't run, I loped along, my eye glued on that descending baseball as it headed for the outstretched glove of the center fielder, who had to run in several steps to catch my utter failure. I didn't run, I stumbled toward first base. It's hard to run with a broken heart.

"Run 'em out, boy! What's wrong with you?" The old scout was yelling. I was halfway to first base before I realized he was screaming at me. Now I could hear him clearly. "Run 'em out, boy. What's wrong with you?"

I had violated a cardinal rule of baseball: run, run as fast as you can, whenever you hit the ball. I could hear the old scout yelling. I understood the words. I knew the rules. I knew why he was shouting. His face was flushed.

He was furious. His anger, honed razor sharp by a lifetime in baseball, cut through the hot, humid air of that summer day.

"Run 'em out, boy. Always run 'em out. You never know what's going to happen in baseball."

I had believed that for years, known that for years. It's true, you never know what's going to happen in baseball. Or in life. But baseball was life. Now in the twinkling of an eye I knew all too clearly what was going to happen in baseball. And in life. My father was right. I wasn't good enough. I wasn't going to play baseball for the New York Yankees. Or the Cardinals. Or anyone. The old man had known all along. Some small part of me must have known that. But I had never accepted it. No, never.

Not good enough. Not play baseball? What in God's name would I do? Work on the assembly line down at the Ford plant? Drive a Manor Bread truck, or a bus, or deliver milk? Work at the post office? That's what the old man had talked up. "For the lucky ones, it's inside work and there's not much heavy lifting; listen, boy, working for the government is pretty good. Ever hear of anyone working for the government getting laid off?"

Could I get on down at Sheffield Steel, make good money, and maybe not lose half of my hearing like my cousins? What about learning a trade? Become an upholsterer, or a bricklayer? Go to barber college or learn watch repair? Now that's something good to know. People are always going to need a haircut or want their watch repaired.

"Run 'em out! Run 'em out, boy!" My dream, my life was swirling down the drain and this old boy was yelling, "Run 'em out."

It was funny, really, when you think about it. Funny-sad. But the insane humor of it all would have been lost on the old, grizzled Cardinals scout, even if he had known, or cared, what it meant for me. Still, I knew what it all meant. Even today I know what it means, and I still can't fully accept the humor in it. Not really.

19

"A Little Polish"

"A little polish, that's what you need," Mom began pronouncing often, midway through my senior year in high school. "That's what anyone needs who's going to amount to something. And that's what a year of college will do. Put a little polish on you, give you a little shine." Her mind was made up; she wasn't about to budge. She held to the value of a little polish as resolutely as she believed in the certainty of the Holy Ghost and the Second Coming.

"When you go over to Monkey Wards or the Jones Store and one of those salesmen walks up to you, you can tell in a second whether he's had some college education," she announced. "There's just something about the way an educated man walks, the way he carries himself, the way he talks. I can spot them every time. The world looks up to men like that. And rewards them, too."

"Known a lot of big shots, have you?" said the voice of darkness. "Successful men shine a little, do they," my father replied more than once to Mom's numerous declarations about the worth of a year of college.

But this time, in the spring of 1957, as graduation loomed menacingly on the horizon, he wasn't spoiling for an argument. He more than agreed about my need for a little polish. It may have been the only thing in the world he and my mother ever agreed upon. But let her ramble on too much about the many obvious successes she had seen and he was likely to tell her, and tell her good, that selling washing machines or refrigerators over at Wards, or being a confident life-insurance salesman, was no great shakes.

"Anybody can do those jobs." She'd better pick a better example of success if she intended to convince anyone that men with a little polish reap great rewards.

"You know good and well what I mean," was her instant reply. "I was just using those as simple examples. Why, a person with a little college can go about as far as he wants."

Lord knows I needed a little shinola. I needed a lot of polish if I was going to shine at anything, even selling shoes at Monkey Wards or a Thom McAn shoe store. That I was utterly lackluster, that I was everything my father thought, started haunting me in the fall of 1956 as I peered forlornly out of the window in high school and remembered that puny fly ball and the fat old Cardinal scout. Harsh truth had its grip around my throat: I wasn't going to play for the Yankees or the Cardinals. It had all been a dream. I had been sleepwalking through life.

All illusions were gone. My trombone had more shine than I did. And I knew, too, as I tooled to and from high school in my 1949 Chevy humming "Muskrat Ramble" or "I Can't Get Started with You" and repeating Jack Teagarden solos note for note, that he could play the trombone—and I couldn't. I was a duffer. Having heard the real thing, I couldn't fool myself.

But go to college? And study? I had never studied anything. Should I for a moment forget that unforgiving fact, Dad could be relied upon to remind me whenever Mom started talking up a year of college. "The only good news," the old man liked to say, "is that you haven't worn your mind out in high school. It'll all be new to you in college, should you go."

He also reminded me, and often, that I didn't know anything. He had me there. What I did know wasn't important. Who cared about the batting averages of Ty Cobb and Babe Ruth, or that Ted Williams was the last ballplayer to hit over .400? Did it matter that I could name the leading pitchers on any big-league team, or spout the dimensions of Yankee Stadium?

And who gave a hoot about being able to discern the many and varied differences between the trumpet styles of "Muggsy" Spanier, Bobby Hackett, and Louis Armstrong? Nobody said, "Come here, kid, I've got a great job for you. You can tell me about the influence of Kid Ory on Turk Murphy." No, it didn't matter that I knew that Teagarden, drunk or sober, could play rings around any other trombone player dead or alive, and that he was part Indian and was, like Mickey Mantle, from Oklahoma.

That was all useless information, right up there with knowing that Bix Beiderbecke was a genius and had died young. And that Bessie Smith was a genius, too, and that no one, nowhere, could lay a glove on her rendition of "Nobody Knows You When You're Down and Out." But that didn't mean spit.

Shakespeare, Milton, Homer, the periodic table of

elements, the causes and battles of the Civil War, the League of Nations, Plato, Aristotle, just where Sarajevo or Seoul is on the map, Beethoven, Mozart, the CCC, D-Day, and the WPA, all that and more, I would learn in time, was knowledge. Glimmers of true learning flashed before my half-open mind, but only glimmers, and I hadn't the foggiest idea what any of that kind of knowledge meant, or even that it had a meaning. What might happen at college was a closed book to me.

College? All I knew was that all the good Northeast High School football players had their hearts set on going to Warrensburg to shine on the gridiron for Central Missouri State Teachers College. And after that they would be men, ready to be high school coaches. The really good players went "over to Lawrence" and played for the University of Kansas Jayhawks or went "down to Columbia" and blocked and punted and passed the ball for the Mizzou Tigers. A friend had heard God call him to be a Baptist preacher, so he was bound for the promised land via William Jewell College in nearby Liberty. Get this: one guy from Northeast went to Yale University. But then everybody knew he was smart as a whip.

The Riding Around Gang was no help. All Gino and Ralphie Joe and the rest could do that spring of 1957 was daydream about the bunch of us taking off for California. Once there, we'd just bum around. "Come on, hell, Delmer's Mercury will get us there." My Chevy wouldn't; it had developed a bad habit of gumming up spark plugs. Anyway, down deep we all knew it was not for the likes of us.

So what to do? We'll get jobs, maybe join the army, see the world, "learn a trade." Go to barber college, learn the old school yell: "cut his cheek, cut his jaw, make his lip, rah, rah, rah."

"Knock if off, will you Ralphie Joe. 'Tain't funny, McGee." Thinking about the future is a drag. "Let's ditch school tomorrow and play Indian ball, play a little penny-ante poker, and we'll forget about it."

Hitting baseballs helped. Shagging fly balls calms a troubled mind wonderfully. Leisurely poker games blurred the line between the dwindling days of spring and the dreaded future. So did cruisin' the drive-ins with the Riding Around Gang. So did the occasional gig with the Bowery Boys. But the future hovered ominously and cast a lengthening, darkening shadow over the last moments of those golden days.

"What about it, what are you going to do? Your mother thinks that a year of college would do you some good." Dad went on to say that he was sure he could help me get on at the Ford plant for the summer, on the assembly line. "Money's good. It'll make a man out of you. Don't worry. You'll feel like going to college after a few days on the line."

He was right. Hands were needed. New car sales were booming—good old Eisenhower prosperity, my father announced to vindicate his voting for Ike the year before. I went to work on the truck assembly line the day after commencement. Lucky me. Welcome to the real world. The work was hard; the day, long. My shift was ten and a half hours a day, with a half hour off for lunch and two fifteen-minute breaks, one in the morning, one in the afternoon. "You get these breaks whether you need them or not," an old-timer told me with a wink.

But the money was great; with overtime pay I was rich as Rockefeller. Dad seemed to be getting smarter every day. This Walter Reuther was a great man. Like the old man, I was a proud, dues-paying member of the UAW, the United Automobile Workers Union.

I bolted motors to truck frames and exhaust pipes to motors. One truck chassis after another rolled along relentlessly. Blink, nod off just a second, and you saw monsters coming at you. "The line will make a man out of you—or kill you," the old guys said. Some of the others, young bucks mostly, came in bragging that they had been out all night, drinking. Each time the line stopped moving, as it oh so rarely did, or their breaks rolled around, they went to sleep instantly. They could sleep standing up.

How did they survive day in and day out? How had the old man stood up to it? No wonder he fell asleep reading the evening paper or headed for bed by 9:30 or so. But what about those times when he and relatives from Wakenda sat on the front porch and talked until all hours of the night? He still had to rise and shine and face the line. No wonder he was grouchy; I now had some understanding of his rage about those awful grade cards I had come home with.

The line numbed the brain. Blink, and you daydream. Veterans of the line delighted in telling me horror stories of men who had nodded off and lost fingers and hands. "Wake up, boy."

One day soon after I went to work, one old worker surprised me by saying, "You can't possibly be Joe's boy, you're too tall." I said I wasn't Joe's boy, that my dad was named Roy. "See, that short man over there, that's my dad."

"That's not Roy, that's Joe," he laughed. When I insisted that I knew my own father, he waved me off good-naturedly saying, "Around here he's Joe."

I'd never heard anyone else ever call him Joe, but that summer everyone in the plant did, and no one seemed to know that his name was anything else. Why they called him that, I don't know. Joe claimed he didn't know either. I never did find out. But I did discover a new side, a happier, lighter side, to the old man. At the plant the guy called Joe smiled often, laughed with his friends, and seemed, well, almost happy-go-lucky. His buddies liked him; with them, he was comfortable and loose, and he had lots of friends.

On the ride home each afternoon I usually saw the grimmer side I knew so well. I usually fell asleep, much to Joe's irritation, but sometimes he melted into mere bemusement at how soft I was.

That summer I had one last fling at baseball, but the combination of an exhausted body and the memory of that dismal fly ball meant that the time for games was over.

So, college. Mom would get her wish. Not Warrensburg, not Mizzou, not KU at beautiful Lawrence, not William Jewell where God-fearing Baptists ruled. I hadn't applied to any of them. It never dawned on me to send for applications. If there was justice in this world I wouldn't have been admitted to any of those schools anyway. No one with a smattering of brains would have bet a nickel on my making it at any college, even at lowly Kansas City Junior College, where I decided to go sometime during the summer of 1957.

Joe/Roy/Dad stood by, not at all convinced that I would last a year, even a semester. But if I was going, he announced, a "college man" needed a proper desk, chair, and desk lamp. I would be living at home, and my bedroom would have to be converted into a place to study—

"You will have to study, you know," Dad said as we walked into the used office equipment store on Truman Road, not far from where Binaggio and Gargotta had gone down in a pool of blood.

A salesman pointed us to a "student desk," one with a file drawer on one side. He also had just the right desk lamp. Now the chair. On this, Dad had fixed opinions. He spied what he had in mind: a sturdy oak chair, that one over there, the one with a curved back. Much of its finish had been worn off, but it was just the ticket. The salesman nodded when my father pronounced it a "banker's chair" and chimed in with, "That chair will outlast us all."

It was the sort, he and my father agreed amiably, you would find in a bank or a courtroom. A good sanding and a couple coats of varnish and it would be as good as new. Joe said he'd take it. The salesman, sizing up his beaming customers, said he'd have to have twenty bucks for the chair, seeing as how it was "real quality." Mom told him, "It's only worth ten, seeing as how it needs refinishing." Would she give fifteen? Done.

So, a banker's chair. We borrowed a neighbor's pickup truck and lugged the furniture home. The chair went right to the basement, where Dad started sanding it that afternoon. Ironically, I had a fine mahogany bookcase I had made in high school wood shop, made as something of a joke. I had two books, a well-thumbed copy of Mark Harris's *The Southpaw* and a fat Webster's dictionary, a graduation present from one of my cousins—other presents had been socks and shirts from Monkey Wards.

I transformed my room. Down came all the photographs of baseball players. In came my new "office furniture" and my dictionary and *The Southpaw*. My new shiny chair gave the room an added luster. By the time classes started my bedroom had been made into a "proper study."

To remind myself of my new mission in life and my barely endured summer at the Ford plant I took a red ballpoint pen and made an impressive sign and taped it to the front of the new desk lamp. "Remember the Assembly Line!" greeted my eye each time I glanced at the desk. I was ready now. Bring on the books, the classes, the "homework."

I ushered my bedazzled mother and bemused father in. Behold the new man. Visions of a shining successful man danced before my mother's eyes. The eternal optimist hugged me and said she knew I could do it. The old man looked around the room, nodded, ran his hand approvingly over the hard, sleek finish on my banker's chair and glanced at my desk lamp. My sign caught his eye. He seemed entranced by it. Surely, now I had his approval.

He looked at me, pointed to the sign in anger, and said coldly, "You've got a long way to go, boy." He walked quickly out of the room. Mom shrugged her shoulders. She had no idea what had set him off. I glanced at the sign, wondering what in the world he could have found to criticize this time. After reading it over a couple of times I discovered the problem. Knucklehead that I was, I had written "Remeber the Assembly Line!" Man, I'll tell you, I had a long, long way to go.

Kansas City Junior College accepted anyone who could make it up the school stairs and brandish a diploma from one of the city's public schools. All you had to do was show up, plop down fifty dollars in tuition, and you were in for a semester. KCJC, or "Junior College," as it was called then, was the college of last resort.

However humble, KCJC crowned the city's public school system. The college, housed in a five-story building at Thirty-ninth and McGee and across the street from Westport High, had no "campus," no rolling hills, no grassy knolls, no tree-shaded commons. There was an old gymnasium in the basement with basketball goals, but little else. There were no sports teams; no dorms; no frat houses; nothing but classrooms and a small library tucked away in a corner of the second floor.

Any bookstore? No, you bought your books—usually one stout textbook per course—across the street at the same store that sold candy and ice cream and textbooks to the high school students. The cafeteria on the fifth floor served the same drab food, in the same prisonlike atmosphere, as did the high schools most of the students had just escaped.

Junior College—there was a people's school, the only public and therefore affordable college in town. It was one last chance for the sons and daughters of barbers and butchers and United Automobile Workers. But this no-frills place actually had teachers who cared, who believed wholeheartedly that working-class children needed an old-fashioned (and required) curriculum of English, history, mathematics, biology, chemistry, physics, psychology. And foreign languages, too—French, German, Spanish. Such learning would transform you forever and help you escape the working class—the primary aim of every student with fifty simoleons for tuition.

Some of the professors, yes sir, had climbed academic Mount Everests and returned certified to put Ph.D. after their names. Most were armed with lesser degrees and had started in the high schools and gained enough seniority or extra academic training to escape to Junior College and wear the mantle "professor." Even the lowliest of the staff approached their classes ready to do battle with ignorance. They were determined to be as rigorous as possible—and to wash out those who shouldn't have been there, or were too thick to learn that this wasn't high school. This was "college." Keep that in mind.

Everyone was terrified of Ray M. Lawless, a little man with a big degree—from the University of Chicago, no less. He was Dr. Lawless to one and all. He had written a book, a real book, and seemed to have read every book known to man or woman. He deserved far better students. Never mind. Five days a week he stood at Armageddon and clobbered his charges with grammar, poetry, essays, short stories, novels—and followed it all up with Friday spelling tests. Yes, old-fashioned spelling tests.

Shirkers and boneheads beware: Dr. Lawless handed out D's and F's liberally and never blinked an eye, at least as far as anyone noticed. "Learn or get out," he stormed. In his second-year course in American literature his charges marched from Puritan sermons and poems to Faulkner and Hemingway novels and short stories. Dr. Lawless demanded that you read *Moby-Dick,* every word of it. And his killer exams made sure that you had gone through every piece of assigned reading with a fine-tooth comb. Learn or get out.

Standing shoulder to shoulder with him was young Arthur Wilkins, tweedy, bespectacled Dr. Wilkins. He was a proud KCJC alum, one of Ray M. Lawless's protégés who'd gone on to the University of Chicago and returned to KCJC because he wanted to teach, "and not be at some impersonal university and grind out essays on second- and third-rate British writers." In his classes, first-rate writers came alive.

Like his mentor, he was all business. He began class by removing his pocket watch and placing it on the lectern by his notes. Not a second to waste. Don't be a fool and come to class unprepared. When Dr. Wilkins called upon you, you'd better know your stuff. There was no getting off with pitiful comments like, "Sorry, Dr. Wilkins, I simply didn't have time to read the assignment."

He was unfazed by such pleas. And utterly unsympathetic. "Go ahead and talk about the poem anyway," Dr. Wilkins replied softly. "Tell your classmates what you think the poet meant."

Surely he hadn't heard. Better speak up. "I'm sorry, sir. I was terribly busy last night, and I just didn't have the time to read the poem. It won't happen again."

"I'm sure it won't," he replied, "but go ahead and enlighten your classmates anyway." He stood there in silence, staring at you. No one spoke a word. Tick, tick, tick. You could hear that infernal pocket watch. Tick, tick, tick, tick. After what seemed an eternity the demanding doctor of philosophy called on someone else. After my first embarrassing run-in with the ticking pocket watch I was never, ever unprepared again.

Mademoiselle Gerardine Knotter strove to civilize her students by drilling French into our heads. She began the moment the bell rang and went full throttle until the end of the hour. She was dead serious about the great battle to drill basic French into her lunkheaded students, many of whom prepped for her afternoon class by playing basketball over the lunch hour in their street clothes and came to class without benefit of a shower or a dry shirt.

No matter. Even the lowliest (and sweatiest) of her students could learn. She was unfailingly cheerful in the face of grubby students like me whose pronunciation would have driven most mortals screaming from the room. If she had shot me point-blank to shut me up forever, a jury of her peers would have acquitted her by acclamation. But no. Any one of us might be saved.

In "Doc" Krekel's European history class you had to listen hard or you might miss the message of salvation, not see the life raft being thrown out. On the surface, Edward Krekel blended bons mots and sarcasm about giants and monsters in the past so nonchalantly a dullard missed his point. To me he was a revelation. History wasn't dates and battles—though his recounting of the Spartan stand at Thermopylae and Napoleon's debacle at Waterloo had even my sleepy classmates holding their breath. History, in Doc Krekel's nimble hands, was people, ideas, causes, consequences, all vividly wrapped together. I was starstruck.

In asides Doc Krekel mentioned Will Durant, Arnold Toynbee, Johan Huizinga, Jakob Burckhardt, saying, as dryly as possible, why don't you check some of these guys out sometime, see what they had to say, then you might understand a little history—you won't if you read only the textbook. I heard the word. And the word was Ed Krekel. I wrote down every word he said. I bought books, lots of books, enough to overflow my spacious bookcase. I began to make lists of titles I would buy and read, someday, if not today. I wanted to have my own books, my own library, like Doc Krekel. How about that!

I began by buying three volumes of Durant's massive, popular history—*The Life of Greece, Caesar and Christ,*

The Age of Faith. These were stout volumes all—in hardback, yet—packed with facts. You talk about good. I loved them. As an ignoramus, fresh from the Ford assembly line, I didn't yet know that I was to despise them because they were "popular history" and pleasures to read. I made the same mistake with Emil Ludwig's *Napoleon.* I loved it, too, even after someone dismissed Ludwig as a lightweight. "You'll be reading Irving Stone next," one of my new highbrow friends joshed.

Occasionally, I did the right thing. I made my way through Huizinga's *The Waning of the Middle Ages.* It was slow going—I read with the speed of cold molasses, but every page yielded prizes. I started Burckhardt's *The Civilization of the Renaissance in Italy,* and swore I'd finish it someday. I kept to my new plan, inspired by Dr. Wilkins, of looking up the definition of every new word I came across. I wrote each on a three-by-five card.

Doc Krekel, Mlle. Knotter, old Dr. Lawless, young Dr. Wilkins, and all of those tending that weedy garden called Kansas City Junior College were overworked and underpaid, I'm sure. Many supplemented their heavy daytime teaching schedules by offering night-school courses. Some moonlighted during vacation by painting houses or working for insurance companies.

Another, a harried instructor in American history, had grueling days on Monday and Wednesdays. On those days he gave the same lecture five times and then twice more in the evening. He remained sane—*if* he remained sane—by reading his lectures, lectures that, everyone in his classes soon learned, were taken word for word from the very textbook we were to read, *The Federal Union* by John D. Hicks.

Our overworked mentor had typed out most of the

great book—this in those ancient days before photo-copying. Wow, we thought: now that's a lot of typing. We marveled more at his herculean effort than at the bizarreness of his lectures. We made allowances for him, reasoning that he must have done this in an earlier day, back before his superiors had selected the text. We joked among ourselves that he seemed so out of it that we doubted whether he knew that his lectures were taken from our book.

This idea inched into our minds. One day he unexpect-edly looked up from his notes, stopped reading, scanned the room with a furrowed brow, and began shouting, "What's wrong with you? Why aren't you taking notes?" Before anyone could think of a way to tell him why we were busy underlining the text as he read along, he blurt-ed out, "This is a college class, remember?"

Then, the tempest passed. He collected himself, looked down at his notes to find his place, and resumed his read-ing. And we went back to underlining the text. Because he was given to abruptly skipping over sections on women or social history of any kind, now and then we had to scramble to find out where he was.

He seldom looked up from his fast-paced reading. (How he would have expected anyone to take notes was a mystery.) If, by some chance, someone had a question or an observation to make, it was necessary to shout out his name to get his attention.

One day someone in the back yelled out his name and said he had a question. It was involved and touched on some contemporary economic injustice. Our teacher lis-tened carefully. He began pacing back and forth. He rubbed his forehead vigorously. He started shaking his head as though he had heard something violently disagreeable. His face turned crimson. Then he let loose with both barrels.

"Capitalism! Capitalism is the enemy," he shouted. Capitalism, the profit motive, private property, excessive rents—all were grinding the poor, the working class, into the mud. He stood with the underprivileged, the oppressed. He lit into greedy factory owners, excoriating the malefactors of great wealth and the corrupt economic system that ground workers down into the mire of poverty. Calamity awaited America, he roared, pointing his finger at some hallucinatory greedy fat cat. He pounded the lectern. He flailed the air with his fists.

We were stunned. No one thought he had any opinions of his own. In his so-called lectures even the illustrations or seemingly off-the-cuff anecdotes came directly from the text. For once he had everyone's undivided attention. Then, he stopped, stopped abruptly. He scanned the room. (How could he miss our stunned expressions?) He looked furtively toward the door as though he expected armed goons from General Motors to come crashing through the door to bloody his head. He removed his glasses, rubbed his eyes. He jerked out a handkerchief and mopped his brow, quickly, nervously. Man, he'd been cookin'.

He mumbled something about having gone too far, having gotten off the subject, and how he hoped we would forgive him. He returned his gaze to his bulging notebook. Slowly, methodically, he began reading his lecture again.

It had been glorious, if a little scary, at least momentarily. Wham! Bazooka blasts had shaken the room. It was his finest hour—or finest five minutes. For an instant our seemingly lobotomized master of history had been fully alive, passionate, speaking his mind, committed to something that he obviously felt willing to storm the barricades for—or at least tell others to. Then, all passion spent, he had scrambled back into the safe, outstretched arms of those cribbed notes.

In the days and weeks to come, we would try to coax the fiery radical hiding inside our Mr. Peepers to come out again and hurl hand grenades at the plutocrats. No such luck. Our questions, hollered out whenever he paused to take a breath or turn the page, crashed and died against his protective shell—his giant notebook. He kept an iron grip on himself. Never again would we have the pleasure of seeing the man flail away at greed and oppression.

The year 1957 was a grand time for a jughead like me to declare (silently, of course), Boneheads Awaken! You have nothing to lose but your chains of ignorance and a world to win! Well, at least to discover. That fall, the Soviets gave the Free World a bop on the ego by launching a man-made satellite into space—the first ever, Moscow crowed. The Ruskies with their *Sputnik*—with a dog aboard, for Chrissake—had jumped out ahead of us in the Space Race. Better do something about that— or we're doomed! Even little tykes were dispatched to their desks to start learning higher math; bigger kids were told to hop to it and study physics and all the other "hard sciences."

Toil and trouble roiled the home front too. That fall, Ike sent troops to neighboring Arkansas to enforce racial integration at Little Rock's Central High School. On television Central High looked disconcertingly like Northeast. And those angry white bobby-soxers and burr-headed white students who taunted and kicked that handful of black kids were familiar. Not even the girls were safe. Their angry tormenters looked embarrassingly like, well, me and the Riding Around Gang, and other good ol' boys I'd known.

The worst good ol' boy, at least in 1957, was right there in Arkansas. Governor Orval Faubus became a symbol of evil, particularly to a young blockhead who now desperately yearned to throw off the chains of ignorance and prejudice and get with the times. It was fun to sit around and mock and curse Orval. This felt a lot better than taunting Old Man Pierce or fretting about the Kansas City A's woeful pitching staff—or continuing to moon over that pitiful fly ball and the moment that had seemed so tragic.

I grew a beard. It was a goatee, actually, and a stringy one at that. But it would have to do. Everyone else was trying to grow a beard to help Castro, and I didn't want to be left behind. Fidel Castro was in the mountains of Cuba shouting revolution at the top of his voice and vowing to topple Batista, the dictator. Then freedom would ring in Cuba. It would be a hard fight, and Fidel needed every bit of support a KCJC freshman could give.

"The Fidelistas have history on their side," someone said, "and Castro will bring democracy." It felt good saying that, believing that. Batista and the whole corrupt lot of hooligans would fall to the bearded Cuban revolutionary. That was the word around KCJC. That was the gospel according to the liberals up on the fifth floor where the bearded crowd hung out, eating our lunches out of brown paper bags.

I did my best to stand shoulder to shoulder with Progress by reading the *New Republic* and tackling a term paper on "The Socialism of Marx and Lenin." I tried to coax that scrawny goatee to thicken out a bit, but it remained recalcitrantly stringy, obscenely so.

My anemic chin whiskers, whatever boost they gave Castro, caused tongues to wag on Thompson Street. The folks on the block, and my legion of cousins and everybody at church, couldn't quite get the hang of how my goatee was helping to bring freedom and justice to Cuba and to bring the world one step closer to universal peace and brotherhood.

It was hard to explain to those who didn't have the advantage of studying at Junior College. Mr. Jim merely smiled; my father, sensing that I was only putting on the agony, putting on the style, seemed bemused. Not Mom. Surely, she said, that peach fuzz on my chin was not the first step toward getting a little polish.

20

Safe at Home

That silly goatee caused no shaking of the foundations of the Home Plate Restaurant. Tucked away off the lobby of the stately Berkshire Hotel, the eatery catered to hotel guests and traveling businessmen grabbing a meal on the run, to secretaries out for lunch, and to shoppers taking a break from their pursuit of good buys on busy Troost Avenue just around the corner. It was a perfect place, with its counter and booths and short-order cooks, to drop in for a quick cup of coffee and a piece of pie. Prices were reasonable. Food was basic, club sandwiches and soups and salads. Service was good. The waitresses ranged in age from eighteen to eighty. It was the sort of place where the cashier, invariably named Gracie or Ruby or Ida, perched on a stool with a cigarette dangling from her lips, laughed long and loud when she damned-well pleased, wore as much makeup as humanly possible, and rather thought her flaming red hair and the half-dozen or so rings on her wrinkled fingers were very stylish and quite appropriate, thank you, for a woman who'd heard every hard-luck story in the book, and had probably fallen for a few of them in her time. But count your change before you leave, mister.

Many of the visiting major-league baseball teams bunked at the Berkshire Hotel when they were in town to play the Kansas City A's. The Home Plate was lavishly decorated with baseball paraphernalia; baseball bats, pennants, photographs of long-gone ballparks and famous ballplayers of years past plus autographed pictures of Mickey Mantle, Bob Feller, Gus Zernial, and other stars of the day festooned the walls and reminded everyone, should they somehow forget it, that baseball was the national pastime. The restaurant did its best late-night business when the Yankees were in town. Customers dropping in around midnight or one o'clock could count on spotting Yogi Berra or the Mick and his buddies, Billy Martin and Whitey Ford, or Moose Skowron, or maybe the Old Professor himself, Casey Stengel, grabbing a snack.

The players obliged the occasionally overzealous fan by enduring a handshake or a pat on the back or by giving an autograph. But one of the glories of the Home Plate was that most of the customers were there for the food or conversation with their friends and usually allowed the ballplayers to eat and unwind in peace. My own emancipation from the one great passion of my youth was so startlingly complete that I never once pestered my former idols for an autograph or felt the need, or the desire, to wave across the room and say, "Way to go, Mick" or "Great game, Moose!" In some strange and unfathomable way, that would have violated my unwritten code for how I was now to behave.

I took to hanging out in the evenings at the Home

Plate, open twenty-fours a day, near the end of my freshman year at KCJC, in the spring of 1958. From the moment I walked in the first time, I was hooked. And for the next year or so while my discovery of history, literature, philosophy, psychology, and good talk soared from that lowly perch, Junior College, I made a nightly pilgrimage to sip the coffee and gulp the magic that was the Home Plate.

I first heard about the charms of the all-night café from Dave, a fellow freshman, a slightly older student who read books. He'd spotted me sitting in the KCJC cafeteria reading D. H. Lawrence's naughty and long-suppressed *Lady Chatterley's Lover* and announced that he was a fan of Lawrence also. I was obviously a kindred spirit. He, too, he announced, read books, even books that weren't assigned in class. He had "a stereo system," the kind with interrelated parts, a far cry from Dad's old primitive record player. Dave talked knowingly about "woofers" and "tweeters" and the importance of properly cleaning one's long-play records.

He had his own apartment and said he considered Handel's "Water Music" good but hardly great. Still, he liked to play it first thing every morning to put him in the mood for classes. Did I agree with him about Handel? I wasn't sure. (Quick, I thought, who is this Handel?) But I wanted to learn. I piped up something about Beethoven's symphonies. (Thank God for the old man and those trips to the Kansas City Philharmonic.)

Dave had traveled a bit and talked casually about exotic places, like New York and California. He'd been "to the coast," knew Los Angeles like the back of his hand, and had bummed around the beaches out there. "Now there is the place to meet beautiful women."

Had I ever been there? No, I said, trying to sound cool, but I'd actually given some serious thought to going. I had, after thinking about it, decided to go to school first. He understood. He dug school, too, though he was inclined to think that the "old Junior College was a bit easy." Don't you? Oh sure. You're right about that, I lied. I had turned into a pencil-head, studying day and night, even recopying the notes I had scribbled in class and checking out the suggested reading to add information to my notes. My shirt pocket bulged with my three-by-five vocabulary cards, which I consulted whenever I had a moment.

I had no choice. I was madly in love with learning now. I was a convert. I burned to learn, to make up for all that lost time hitting baseballs and staying in good standing with the Riding Around Gang. Also, I was dumber than anyone could imagine. But my new suave, sophisticated friend didn't need to know that.

I certainly didn't tell him that soon after arriving at the "old Junior College," I was called to the guidance counselor's office. Every freshman received a note to stop by, and I showed up with Tommy and Howard, a couple of buddies from Northeast. The counselor, the soul of earnestness, looked up and said that since we were friends the three of us might as well come into her office together. She had received the results of the standardized tests we'd taken the first day of school. This test, "taken by entering college freshmen all over the United States," was not an intelligence test. She wanted us to know that. But it was a pretty good indicator of "success in college." Our scores were in percentiles with 100 being the top, "though nobody ever makes that." No, "good scores," for KCJC students, were around the fiftieth percentile.

She opened Howard's booklet, looked consolingly at him, and said he hadn't done too badly. His score was in the forties. "Now that means that just slightly more than half of all the people who took this test did better." Howard, known more for his prowess on the football field than for his work in the classroom, was pleased.

"Now, Tommy. Let's look at how you fared. Perhaps you scored even higher." His score was much better. That pointed to a bright future. He flushed a bit from embarrassment. Tommy already knew what he wanted to be, a pharmacist—"just like Old Man Pierce," we kidded him—and that score told him something pretty important. Howard and I weren't surprised. Tommy, gangling and unathletic, had been a good student and, as my mother would say, "had success written all over him."

Now for my score. It wouldn't be up there with Tommy's—he was known to be extra smart—but it would probably be as good as Howard's. Our counselor smiled, opened my test booklet, and. . . her face turned to stone. After a long moment and a sigh, she looked up at me and then back at the score. "Excuse me," she said in a barely audible voice, "we really ought to go over these marks in private."

I agreed amiably. I guessed I hadn't scored quite as high as Howard and certainly nowhere near Tommy's mark. I nodded a casual good-bye to my buddies and told the counselor to "fire away."

There was no easy way she could break the news to me, she said. Could it be that some mistake had been made in calculating my percentile score? No, she didn't think so. "The machines that grade these exams don't make mistakes." She stared at me in wonderment.

"I hate to tell you this," she said as consolingly as possible, "but your score is . . . , well, three." That's right, three!

My dumb look gave me away. I didn't know what a three meant. She explained it haltingly, searching for words. "This means that 97 percent of all the people in the entire United States who took this exam did better than you." Having said that she simply stared at me, her face growing crimson. Her shocked silence, I think, was not that I had made such an abysmal score, but that the moron sitting in front of her was actually enrolled in college.

"Well," I told her with a big smile, "I know what to do."

What was that, she wanted to know, the red from her cheeks slowly subsiding, the tremble gone from her voice. She was probably hoping that I would say I would quit, leave school that instant, and make straight for the Ford plant or barber college.

"The next time I take a test like that," I told her confidently, "I'll pick the answer I think is right, and then actually check any other choice. That means I could make a score of ninety-seven."

She sat in stunned silence as I rose, said good-bye, and walked out the door to catch up with my friends, who were lurking in the hall.

"You're just ignorant enough to think that's possible," Howard joshed as we made straight for the cafeteria to grab a Coke before class. Howard was right about my ignorance, though I bragged that the test hadn't been a complete waste of time, that I had left the examination room and looked up the first word in the vocabulary section. I now knew what *filch* meant. Did they?

But that score filched some of my innocence and rattled around in my head from that day on. It was one of the things that reminded me to study, and study hard. That Big Little Three screamed, "Buster, you've got miles to go"—in the classroom, in the library, in the bookstore, or in my banker's chair at my desk back on Thompson Street—before you ever catch up with the Howards and Tommys of this world.

It was one thing for them to know my score. They thought it was a great joke. I joined them in laughing heartily at my miserable mark. But inwardly I grimaced every time I thought about it. And it would be better, I told myself, to keep that lowly three to myself around my new KCJC friends like Dave, who pronounced some things "inexplicable" or "anachronistic," words I scrambled to find in the dictionary and scribbled on a card the moment the coast was clear.

"Do you ever go to the Home Plate?" Dave asked one day. "It's not far from school. Right near the corner of Troost and Linwood." He often grabbed a sandwich there before going to work—he was "on his own," I learned, and sacked groceries every evening from five to eleven. But come quitting time he headed for the Home Plate to study or have good conversation. "Some amazing characters show up there most evenings."

When no one interesting came around or he was too tired to study he grabbed a booth, ordered coffee, and opened his copy of Dostoevsky's *Crime and Punishment*. Had I ever read it? No, but it was "on my list of great books to read." Actually, Dave said, he hadn't read it either, and would probably never get through it at the rate he was going. But he had found that women ("particularly the kind I like to meet") were impressed when they discovered a man reading a big book. It didn't have to be Dostoevsky; it could be Thomas Mann or Tolstoy, "but not Shakespeare or someone like Chaucer." They scared women, even brainy types, he'd discovered.

The trick was to make it all look natural. "Don't appear to be sweating over the damned thing. And don't, for God's sake, underline the book. That puts women off." Sit down, open the book casually; don't hurry. Always be cool. Read, or pretend to read ("it really doesn't matter"), a few pages. Look up from time to time, nod to yourself as though you are thinking deep thoughts, then look around the room. "Remember, man, be cool." And don't overdo the nodding part.

When I laughingly reminded him that I "had a girl" and was "serious" and was going to marry her, he said everyone has a high school sweetie, and that I would get over her once I saw what the big world had to offer. He intended to continue playing the field. I could watch—and suffer.

I didn't suffer at the Home Plate. I was there for the intellectual buzz Dave had promised. He flirted with the waitresses and every woman who looked "interesting." Women of all ages loved him in spite of that slightly receding hairline; one told me he was "a handsome dog." The bejeweled cashier, Ida, still young at heart, matched him step for step in the flirting department, telling him more than once that he was welcome to come over to her place some night and look at some old books she had. He was right, dead right, about the importance of at least appearing earnest about, say, *Crime and Punishment* or *War and Peace* or some other big book.

But he let me be on the matter of wooing women. Anyway, he wanted to talk about books. He had read enough of Dostoevsky and Tolstoy to impress me, and he was a great talker. I tested him once. He made a passing reference to D. H. Lawrence and I challenged him, only to discover that he had read *Lady Chatterley's Lover* closely and was prepared to talk at length about the gamekeeper and Lawrence's sexually frustrated heroine and her lame husband.

He knew Plato, too, or as much as I did. I was taking a course in philosophy and struggling with *The Republic.* Many pages and whole sections required two or three readings, and even then I wasn't exactly sure I understood anything about philosopher-kings and how only the "idea" of the state was true, or knowable. I took notes; I copied out long sections; I wore out my paperback dictionary looking up strange words. Somewhere along the way Dave had read Plato—and understood him. He even knew why everybody made a big fuss about the differences between Plato and Aristotle. When I reminded him of what he'd said was the real reason he carried big books around with him, he laughed and said that sometimes pretty girls weren't around, or "didn't dig intellectuals," and he'd found himself actually reading the book that lay open before him.

"But if we want to talk philosophy, or anything important, we need to talk to that guy over there," said Dave, pointing to a slightly burly guy across the restaurant who was absorbed in a book and smoking a pipe. "That's Ed, a real philosopher, and not one of those peckerwoods at Junior College."

It turned out that Ed was the real thing. I had never met anyone like him. He not only knew everything about philosophy, he knew lots about everything—history, politics, literature, ideas from the ancient past, and what was in that day's newspaper. He was informed about things Asian. Buddha and Confucius: he could talk about them. He knew Zoroastrianism. Saint Augustine's *Confessions* was a great book, he reckoned, even if it was written by a Christian, but it wasn't as important to modern readers as *The Confessions of Jean-Jacques Rousseau.* The names of Nietzsche and Marx and two Americans, William James and John Dewey, cascaded from his lips as easily as bromides and Bible verses poured out of my mother or Bro. Roger Rinkenbaugh. My teachers at KCJC were hardly peckerwoods, but some were close to being popguns compared to Ed, sage in residence at the Home Plate every night from 11:00 P.M. to whenever.

Who was the mysterious Ed? Where had he come from? How had he gotten to be so smart? And why wasn't he a teacher, a professor, or a writer? God knows he could have been a brilliant teacher.

He was slightly muscular. Somewhere in his early thirties, he looked like a light heavyweight contender and carried himself in a manner that said don't mess with me. That book tucked under his arm or spread out before him at the Home Plate said he preferred to think and be left alone. He had thick black wavy hair, and there was something about the intense look in his eyes and the square jaw that put me in mind of Van Heflin or John Hodiak. He gave off a trace of sadness.

He didn't like to talk about himself—he preferred to talk philosophy—but I pried enough out of the waitresses to get a fair idea of who he was and what had gone wrong and why he preferred the shadowy half-life of the Home Plate after dark.

Ed drove a cab. Starting around 10:30 or so each morning, he began a twelve-hour shift and worked seven days a week. Afterward, he made his way to the Home Plate to read for three or four hours. "That's all he wants to do," said an amused waitress old enough to be Ed's mother. He had attended New York University and was about to graduate with a major in philosophy when the Korean War broke out and Ed was drafted, or joined. Some thought he had been in the army, others swore he had been a marine. He didn't get wounded or anything, but his best friend had been shot up pretty bad and died. And if that wasn't enough, Ed had received a Dear John letter from his fiancée. Or it may have been his wife. "Anyway," someone at the Home Plate told me, "when he got out of the service he said to hell with everything—school, the rat race, everything, even old friends. He just came to Kansas City and tried to disappear."

When asked by waitresses or young female customers of a marriageable age if he didn't "want to go back to school and get a degree and get a good job," Ed said no and picked up his book. If they continued to pester him, he replied softly that "good" was a concept certainly worthy of discussion, and that he had thought about it a fair bit and concluded that he had a "good" job, maybe, given everything, one of the best in the world. That usually sent the frustrated young women on their way.

"I think he's one of them beatniks, but he wouldn't hurt a fly," one middle-aged waitress volunteered to me one night before Ed arrived.

A beatnik? No, I didn't think so. They were usually scrawny, odd-looking types with goatees—I had prudently shaved mine—and didn't work and slept all day and wore berets and dark T-shirts and smoked brown Turkish cigarettes and insisted their coffee be thick as mud and black as the ace of spades and made in funny-looking machines. Beatniks sat around in restaurants with the windows painted black and recited poetry that didn't rhyme. One proclaimed beatnik I knew fancied a flavored iced-coffee concoction called a "Mint Cool Lip."

Ed drank his coffee straight and said philosophy was poetry, though he had started reading someone named Rainer Maria Rilke—"How do you spell that name, Ed?"—who had a great deal to say. When I asked him about D. H. Lawrence, he shrugged. When questioned about Jack Kerouac and Allen Ginsberg he said he'd read *On the Road* and had a friend who'd heard Ginsberg read *Howl* but that he preferred Rilke. "If you like Lawrence or Keroauc, read them."

Ed seemed to have read everything, though he continued to come back to Spinoza. The man died before he had a chance to develop all of his ideas fully, Ed insisted. But while he lived he wrote enough—Ed's favorite was Spinoza's *Ethics*—to show how ideas work and could be proved rationally through axioms and theorems with geometrical precision. They in turn made the world understandable. When Ed got wound up, as he often did when explicating a passage from Spinoza, most of what he said sailed high above my head. Apparently Spinoza had taken Descartes and improved on him by showing that everything is One. Everything: our minds, our ideas, the world around us, is One. What some call Nature is One.

This was Monism, Ed explained. I had heard that slippery word at school and couldn't pretend to get a firm grip on it, but I knew that in the great debate about whether the world is One or Many, Ed and his man Spinoza had come down hard on this thing called monism, something we could understand through reason.

Did that have anything to do with something called God, I asked one night. "It has everything to do with God," Ed explained, but not in the way I used the word. As someone who was now suspicious of all God talk, I listened carefully to what Ed had to say, but I didn't understand what he meant about God. There was much he said that I didn't understand. No matter. What I took in, even the very difficult, confusing parts, was manna from my new heaven.

It wasn't always Spinoza's theorems or axioms. Ed was a fountain of information about John Locke, Hegel, Nietzsche (not one of Ed's favorites, any more than Freud was). He held John Dewey in high regard, said he understood Reason. Ed was passionately ambivalent about William James, but I can't remember why, or what he said. It doesn't—and didn't—matter. Sitting across the table from Ed night after night and hearing him hold forth or trying to answer his questions about any assertion I made was sheer magic. When everything else has fled from my mind, even my name, my memory of my once youthful face, even Ted Williams's 1941 batting average, and Mr. Jim's sunny smile, or the cadence of church hymns, some small part of me will continue to vibrate to the beat of those late-night seminars. Under the tutelage of Ed, the Home Plate was my Ivy League, my Oxford, my Sorbonne. Here was a true college education. No tuition. No reading assignments. No exams. Just learning.

Ed held to Spinoza and the consolations of philosophy with the passions of a medieval monk, or a rabbinical scholar. He talked often of Spinoza being a Jew and how he was "too religious in the larger sense" for his synagogue. Ed, too, was religious in the largest sense possible.

Did he ever succumb to some prejudice, petty or grand? Not in my presence. In everything his mind touched, he was the soul of kindness, of generosity of spirit.

The loyal late-nighters at Ed's table were taking an advanced seminar on multiculturalism, long before the word was blowing in the wind. Blacks mingled with whites; grocery-store sackers supped with philosophers; Dostoevsky devotees flirted with waitresses; fans and famous ball players waved obligingly to each other; and everyone there danced to the music of humanity.

Each night, usually around one-thirty in the morning, a group of gay men—in those days always pronounced "Ho-mo-Sexuals" by all Kansas Citians I knew— dropped in for coffee or a meal. They usually picked a table in a corner. Several wore dresses or, in summer, very short shorts; the rest preferred colorful silk shirts or billowy sweaters, and most had jewelry dangling from their necks or wrists, and sometimes their ears. They came from the Colony Club, a bar around the corner on Troost Avenue. Some of them were female impersonators; some may have been "Hetero-Sexuals." Whatever, they laughed and talked and socialized with the waitresses or anyone who cared to pull up a chair and talk, though few outsiders joined their circle.

Ed occasionally took a seat among them when one of their number began a poetry reading. They didn't make a fuss. Amid the din of clattering coffee cups and the ringing of the cash register they would sometimes read Whitman, Ginsberg, or Kenneth Rexroth aloud. They read softly; one had to concentrate to hear. Sometimes the entire restaurant quieted momentarily and everyone strained to hear the lines. Now and then someone or more applauded—"the poem, not those queers," a stranger in the next booth whispered to me one night.

There may have been others, many others, who felt that way and made nasty comments. I wasn't too far downriver from days when I had spewed vulgarities of all description—or listened approvingly. But now I watched Ed and tried to emulate the man, even down to the expression on his face. I took to puffing on a pipe—though it can't be said that I actually mastered the smoking bit—and made promises to myself to read Spinoza and Rilke someday.

One night Ed said he wanted Dave and me to meet his friend Dick. Dick had wandered in with a wild look in his eye and a giant notebook under his arm. Pencils and ballpoint pens of every size and description bulged from his pockets. He sat down and immediately started jabbering about Time, the "so-called fourth dimension," and how he could now prove—"let's see, I've got it all laid out in my notebook"—the existence of a fifth dimension and perhaps more, a sixth and seventh. Theorems and geometrical designs danced constantly in his head—maybe that was one of the reasons Ed listened to him as carefully as he listened to me or Dave. With his red, green, and yellow pens and his protractor, Dick had worked it all out and could show conclusively that the fifth dimension rolled back on itself and penetrated the fourth.

The man was stark raving mad. His clothes were filthy; his hair shot out in all directions. He was a stranger to a bar of soap or a bathtub. But Ed greeted him warmly, asked him to sit down, introduced him to everyone at the table, and said, "Let's have a look at those drawings." Dick handed him page after page of intricate designs bristling with arrows and circles within circles, each page a kaleidoscope of all the colors in the rainbow.

Dick came in regularly but frequently preferred to sit by himself and probe time and space and other dimensions only he saw. On such occasions, he went straight to his table, opened his notebook, and went to work for hours, looking up only to slurp his coffee. Other times, he joined us, sometimes not saying a word, often dozing peacefully. The waitresses served him all the coffee he wanted and never once gave him a bill. Sometime later I learned that Ed settled up regularly with the cashier for Dick's expenses.

Periodically, Dick disappeared and was nowhere to be found for weeks. I asked Ed about him once. He said that his friend had been taken to some hospital. But I was not to worry. "This has happened lots of times in the past. Dick will be out one of these days and he'll be back."

Sure enough, Dick returned. His hair was neatly trimmed. He was clean-shaven. His suit coat was of another day and slightly too big for his scrawny frame, but it was clean and pressed. He then calmly explained that he had been in the "loony bin" but that he was not nuts and that he had been able to convince his doctors. "How in God's name did you do that?" I blurted out.

Easy, Dick said, scanning the room to see who might be listening. He wasn't offended by my rude question. "I get real chummy with my doctor and ask him all sorts of questions about nutty people and what causes them to go bonkers." Doctors, Dick had learned, loved to talk about themselves, especially to someone who had a keen interest in what they were doing, particularly their pet theories. Dick then took himself to the hospital library and read everything he could find by their favorite authorities. "After that it's duck soup," said Dick. He adroitly told the doctors what they wanted to hear—that is, what they believed. After a while, they said this man's not insane—a little off center maybe, but not crazy. He's certainly not going to harm anybody or himself. Many of them pronounced him a brilliant eccentric.

"Works every time," Dick smiled, his eyes twinkling. He had me halfway convinced that he couldn't be loony if he could do all that. For a while he appeared as normal as was possible for him. Then he returned with his eyes blazing, his notebook bulging with intricate drawings, his pockets jammed with colored pens and pencils, and wild talk about seeing through space. It's all here in my notebook. Did we want to see it? It was always just a question of time before he would disappear again. Ed always said he hoped Dick was okay.

Dick the lunatic; Ed the taxicab philosopher; the ballplayers, Moose and Whitey; the bejeweled gays; Dave the Dostoevsky man; Ida and Gracie the amused cashiers; all felt safe at home. I felt safe at home, too. Finally.

Afterword

"You don't look back along time but down through it, like water," says Magaret Atwood. "Sometimes this comes to the surface, sometimes that, sometimes nothing. Nothing goes away." Margaret Atwood got it right. In writing this book I found that nothing had gone away, not completely. The past of my boyhood refuses, thank goodness, to sink forever beneath the waters of my memory. I see, feel, hear, even smell those bygone boyhood days in Kansas City. Mr. Jim's sitting in his chair, Dad's still haunted by Buck, Mom's fixing to go to church, Old Man Pierce is still honked off about that orange concentrate, Ed's sitting at the Home Plate reading Spinoza, the Mick's young, and so am I—and I am still dreaming about hitting baseballs and playing the trombone like Jack Teagarden.

In the words of Missouri's famous son Mark Twain, this book tells the truth, mainly. No, make that mostly. I have here and there changed the names of some folks to protect the innocent. But other than that, this book tells the truth as best as I can about a time now gone.

The following either helped jog my memory, told me

stories so true I had to listen, asked me questions I (sometimes) tried to dodge but couldn't, read parts or all of this book, or just listened to me ramble on: Judith and Michael Bassett; John, Mari, and Emma Clayton; Sarah Clayton; Kenneth Van Deusen; John Egerton; Fred Frank; Jennifer, Alex, Samuel, and Anna Gelman; David Hart; Jonathan Helmreich; Lela and John Hendrix; Fred Hobson; Robert Hohner; Jackie and Nels Juleus; Jane Lago; Brian Meggitt; Carin and Michael Piraino; John Salmond; Barry Shapiro; Jerry Stephens; Horace Stoessel; Paula Treckel; Richard Turk; Donald Vrabel; Jane Westenfeld; Arthur Wilkins; TaMarra Woodling; and Beth, Paul, Daniel, Frances, and Madelon Visintainer. I owe a very special thanks to my sister, Leila Smith, whose wonderful laugh and good memory helped more than she knows; to Roy Beaty and Lyle Dorsett, good friends from way back whose recollections were invaluable; to the best editor a writer could have, Beverly Jarrett; and to the best wife any man could have, Carrah Hendrix Clayton.

The responsibility for any single word or idea of this account, however, lies exclusively with me.

About the Author

B ruce Clayton is Harry A. Logan Sr. Professor of History at Allegheny College in Meadville, Pennsylvania. He is the author or editor of several books, including *Forgotten Prophet: The Life of Randolph Bourne*, which is available from the University of Missouri Press, and *W. J. Cash: A Life*.